Keep This
Toss That

The Practical Guide to Tidying Up

Updated and Expanded Edition

JAMIE NOVAK

Reader's Digest

New York, NY/Montreal

A READER'S DIGEST BOOK

Photographs reprinted with permission from the following: front cover (top), deryabinka/Shutterstock; front cover (bottom), New Africa/Shutterstock; back cover (top), Kidsada Manchinda/Shutterstock; back cover (bottom), vilax/Shutterstock

Illustrations on pages 155, 274, 281, 284, 285, 287, 291, and 293 courtesy of The Noun Project.

All other illustrations by Ruth Yoel

Library of Congress Cataloging-in-Publication Data
Novak, Jamie.
 Keep this, toss that : unclutter your life to save time, money, space, and sanity / Jamie Novak. -- 1st Edition.
    pages cm.
Includes index.
 Summary: "Quick answers to the one key question everyone needs to answer in order to get organized and save their time, money, space, and sanity: "Should I keep or toss this?""-- Provided by publisher.
ISBN 978-1-62145-475-5 (paperback) -- ISBN 978-1-62145-216-4 (epub)
1. Storage in the home. 2. Time management. I. Title.
TX309.N6856 2015
648'.8--dc23
                         2014038314

We are committed to both the quality of our products and the service we provide to our customers.
We value your comments, so please feel free to contact us.
    Reader's Digest Adult Trade Publishing
    44 South Broadway
    White Plains, NY 10601

For more Reader's Digest products and information, visit our website:
    www.rd.com (in the United States)
    www.readersdigest.ca (in Canada)

Printed in the United States of America

10 9 8 7 6 5 4 3 2 (paperback, original edition)

10 9 8 7 6 5 4 3 2 1 (paperback, updated and expanded edition)

NOTE TO OUR READERS

This book is proof that you're not alone!
If you've lost your dining room table under a pile of mail;
shoved stuff in a bag and hid it before company came over;
or you save the "good" shopping bags with the rope handles,
then we'll be great friends.
I'm honored to support you as you toss stuff to create a home
you feel good about—so good, you'll want to keep it
clutter-free forever! This book is for you, my friend.

Contents

Introduction **vii**

Will This Work for Me? • Keep/Toss Questions • Your Quick-Start Guide

> **SPECIAL FEATURE:**
> *Sidestep Decluttering Stumbling Blocks x*

Chapter 1:
ENTRYWAY AND MUDROOM **1**

Everyday Essentials • In Your Over-the-Door Organizer • Outdoor Gear

> **SPECIAL FEATURE:**
> *16 Clever Ways to Repurpose an Over-the-Door Shoe Organizer 10*

Chapter 2:
BATHROOMS AND COSMETICS **20**

Body Care • Skin Care and Antiaging Products • Spa Products • Hair Care • Nail Care • Cosmetics • First Aid and Medication

Chapter 3:
CLOSETS AND LAUNDRY AREA **41**

Laundry • Cleaning Supplies • Tools and Cords • Linen Closet • Hall Closet • Pet Supplies

> **SPECIAL FEATURE:**
> *In Case of Emergency, Be Prepared—and Organized! 55*

Chapter 4:
FAMILY AND LIVING ROOM **70**

Entertainment • Decor

Chapter 5:
KITCHEN AND DINING ROOM **80**

Appliances • Pots and Pans • Cooking Utensils • Dishes and Serving Ware • Food • Cooking References • Cooking and Dining Accessories

> **SPECIAL FEATURES:**
> *7 Essential Cooking Utensils 90*
> *Let's Play the Gadget Game 94*

Chapter 6:
BEDROOMS AND CLOTHING **116**

Bedroom Furniture and Accessories • Clothing • Jewelry and Accessories

> **SPECIAL FEATURE:**
> *The F's and S's of Clothes to Keep* **128**

Chapter 7:
KIDS' ROOMS   140

Toys and Games • Books • Furniture and Decor • Clothing

Chapter 8:
STORAGE SPACES, GARAGE, AND CAR 154

In the Attic and Basement • In the Garage • In the Car

Chapter 9:
OUTDOOR SPACES   165

Balcony, Porch, and Patio Items • Outdoor Accessories • Gardening and Landscaping Supplies • Pool

Chapter 10:
OUTINGS   178

Sightseeing/Vacation • Day Trips • Beach/Lake/Pool/Picnic

Chapter 11:
CRAFTING AND HOBBIES   188

Crafting Supplies

Chapter 12:
SPORTS AND ACTIVITIES   198

Ball-Centered Sports and Games • Billiards • Bowling • Yoga/Exercising/Weight Lifting • Walking/Running • Gymnastics/ Dance • Music • Fishing • Outdoor Games and Lawn Activities • Biking • Surf/Body/ Paddleboarding • Skiing/Snowboarding • Hiking/Camping

Chapter 13:
KEEPSAKES AND PHOTOGRAPHS   222

Print Photographs • Memorabilia • Memento Clothing • Ceremonial Clothing • Household Items • Assorted Inherited Items

SPECIAL FEATURES:
Children's Keepsakes 227
Collections 240

Chapter 14:
OFFICE   243

Home Office • Corporate Office

Chapter 15:
PAPERWORK   253

Personal Documents and Records • Financials • Everyday Papers and Junk Mail

SPECIAL FEATURES
How Long Do I Really Need to Keep This Paperwork? 258
Paperwork for Children with Special Needs 264
Kitchen Paperwork 268

Chapter 16:
DIGITAL LIFE 277

Computer Files • Downloads & DVR
Recordings • Email and Social Media
• Smartphones

Chapter 17:
CLUTTER CHALENGES 279

Change in Housing • Loss of a Loved One
• Getting Your Affairs in Order • Change in
Living Arrangements • Change in Ability •
Change in Storage Options

SPECIAL FEATURES:
*When Your Family No Longer Wants the
    Family Heirlooms 286*
*When You've Been the Storage Space
    for Someone Else 294*

Conclusion: 284

What's Your Why? • Toss Those Clutterbug
Excuses

Appendix A:
How to Toss Things 301

Appendix B:
Where to Toss Things 303

Keep in Touch with Me 306

INTRODUCTION

Welcome to the feel-good organizing book! I'm so glad you're here. Are you ready to feel good:

- knowing you're not the only one with too much stuff
- laughing about all the silly things you keep
- making mindful choices about what you hold onto
- passing your unused items to someone who will benefit from having them
- about your home for the first time in a long while

Can you already tell this isn't any ordinary organizing book? Instead of wasting time labeling and alphabetizing your spices, let's just toss the ones you don't use (and the ones that expired three years ago). I know you have better things to do than sort stuff. And I bet you'd have a lot less clutter if you could actually decide what to keep and what to toss. You want to be organized, but when your head says "toss" and your heart says "keep," you put it off until later, only later never comes.

So, let's stop pretending; promising yourself you'll finish that craft project, telling yourself you'll wear that sweater that still has a tag on it, or imagining you might finally prepare that recipe you clipped out of the magazine a year ago.

You're saving stuff for a life you are not living, and all that clutter causes you to miss out on life today. Are you ready to experience the relief that comes with lifting the weight of the clutter, losing the guilt and regret, eliminating the feeling of being discouraged and overwhelmed by the stuff? No more excuses. If you've had enough, then get ready to keep this and toss that!

Will This Work for Me?

Written for those of us with too much stuff and not enough time, I've devised a simple checklist method for deciding which items to keep and which to toss. Whether you are a renter, recently moved into your first home, moved into your home five years ago (but just haven't unpacked all the boxes yet), or have forty years' worth of accumulated stuff in your home, the Keep/Toss Checklists will work for you! They'll also work if you're overly sentimental, merging your household with a new spouse or partner, preparing to welcome home a new baby, cleaning out a home you inherited, or downsizing your empty nest.

My easy-to-follow Keep/Toss Checklists take all the guesswork, fear, guilt, regret, and frustration out of what could be a daunting process. And they are easily customizable to suit your space and your lifestyle. Only you know for sure if you make waffles every Sunday and need to keep your trusty waffle iron, but I know no one needs to keep

eleven nonrefillable pens that no longer write! The keep/toss process is not about buying more but about looking at what you already own, considering what you really need, then keeping the best and tossing the rest. (Oh, and by "toss," I mean don't necessarily mean throwing it into the trash. You can "toss" something by donating, selling, recycling, or trading it in. More on that in Appendices A and B.).

Some tosses are obvious. These are the things that have a layer of dust on them, the items you've known you need to toss but you just haven't gotten around to it yet. Of course, you should toss any kitchen utensil that has melted, bent, warped, peeled, rusted, flaked, or can't be repaired. I'll prompt you to finally get rid of all the stuff that's been driving you crazy.

Other tosses are less obvious. These are all the items you've kept out of habit, obligation, or "just in case" you'll need it one day. In this book, I'll help you determine which items are really just clutter and can therefore be tossed without regret.

And then there are the keepers. These are the items you love or love to use regularly. They suit your current style, make your life easier, or just make you happy! They are easy to clean, in good working order and simple to store, and oftentimes serve multiple purposes. I'll tell you how you can get even more joy out of your favorite things by pointing out other uses for them. Along the way be on the lookout for:

KEEP/TOSS CLUE: Hints to help you think through choices about your clutter.

STORAGE SOLUTION

Smart storage ideas you probably never thought of.

Did you know?

Little fun facts to keep you in the know.

We don't all have the same size homes with the same rooms and the same clutter. And we all have different interests, hobbies, and lives. So how can the same lists work for everyone? The Keep/Toss Checklists are designed to cover a wide variety of scenarios.

Start with the basic lists. Where applicable, there are suggested additions or subtractions to the lists based on your lifestyle. If you camp on the weekends, you need camping gear. If you have school-age children, they need backpacks. But if you haven't camped in seven years, you can reconsider your musty tent. And if your kids are off to college, you don't need to hang on to their character-themed backpacks. This book should be useful to you today, tomorrow, and long after that. As you, your family, home, hobbies, and career change, revisit the lists.

Sidestep Decluttering Stumbling Blocks

1. But I don't have time.
Now is the time to put yourself at the top of your to-do list. You deserve a home you are proud of. To make that happen, you just need to carve out ten minutes here and there.

2. But I lack motivation.
Schedule a donation pickup by a local organization. Once you have a deadline, you are more likely to get things done. Or reserve something you enjoy, like listening to a podcast, and only allow yourself to listen while or after you toss.

3. But first, I need supplies and a plan.
Without this book, that might be true. But you now have a plan. And ideas for how to store things using things you already own.

4. But it'll never be perfect.
It doesn't have to be. Make your home work for you, and stop comparing it to unattainable photos on the cover of home magazines.

5. But if I can't finish it all, why even start.
Moving a project forward at any speed is a success. Focus on small consistent successes; soon, they will add up to a finished project.

6. But I don't have any space where I can sort stuff.
Try to find one large item to move to create space. It's okay if you temporarily need to make a bigger mess. Reserve the last few minutes of your ten-minute session for putting things away.

7. But I'm overwhelmed.

Taking action is always the best remedy when you feel like it is all too much. Do a little something, and watch how you shift from feeling like it's too much to being energized by your progress.

8. But I keep getting distracted.

It can happen. You're in the middle of tossing and you find something that catches your eye; before you know it, you are down a rabbit hole. Setting a timer helps keep you on track.

9. But I overthink my decisions.

Don't waver. Trust you made a good choice. Then get the bag of tosses out of your house before you're tempted to take things out of the bag.

10. But I live with a saver/collector.

If you and your spouse, parent, child, roommate, or anyone else sharing your space disagree about what constitutes clutter, it can make organizing doubly difficult. Try teaming up with the person to each find items to give away. Agree on guidelines for what can be tossed—for example, any newspaper more than one year old. And focus on controlling your own clutter; sometimes that can motivate the other person to clean up theirs.

Keep/Toss Questions

Through the years, I've identified three questions that can help you determine whether an item is a keeper. Answering these honestly helps you get a clear indication of whether or not the item is something you can toss.

1. **Do I love it enough to let something else go to make space to keep it?**

This question helps you weigh the item's value to you, most helpful when deciding about keepsakes and decor. For example, if you have two plastic storage tubs to store holiday decorations and your new musical snow globe won't fit, then you should only keep it if you love it enough to let go of something else, like the crumbling door wreath, to make space for it.

2. **Do I love to use it?**

If you have multiples of this type of item, keep the one that makes you happiest or your life easiest. This question best applies to clothing and utilitarian items, like toiletries or kitchen appliances. For example, if you own three garlic presses, keep the one that works easily and toss the one that has lots of tiny holes that are a pain to clean and the one that has a cover you can never snap on.

3. **Do I have a duty to keep it?**

This applies mostly to paperwork and important documents. If it is a required item, like a tax document or birth certificate, and you are expected to keep your own copy, then you have to find a safe place to store it.

Need more help figuring out what to toss and what to keep? In each chapter, you'll find more questions that are specific to different categories of stuff.

Also, ask yourself these three questions before you bring anything new into your house, lest you create more clutter and derail all the great progress you've made in tidying up.

Your Quick-Start Guide

If you're ready to be clutter-free, here's how you can get started.

Work chapter by chapter: When you're already overwhelmed by the clutter, trying to decide where to begin might just stop you in your tracks. That's not what I want for you. Therefore, I've arranged the book chapters in the order in which I suggest you go through your home.

We'll begin in the entryway, and I know what you're thinking. But Jamie, I haven't been able to walk in my walk-in clothes closet for a while, things topple out of the kitchen cabinets, and I have tubs of photographs to sort—yet you want me to start at the front door?

Yes, I do. A calm and welcoming entryway sets the tone for your whole house. It's also the first space company sees when they stop by, so if you've been leaving your company on the porch, you'll now be able to invite them inside. The entryway is the perfect place to find a few quick tosses, immediately creating needed storage space. The idea is to start with easier spots, like the bathroom,

since there's no debating expired tubes of ointment. This lets you practice your decision-making skills as you gradually work up to the more challenging categories. By the time you get to later chapters with things like clothing clutter, sentimental treasures, and piles of paperwork, you'll feel confident about your choices.

Or jump ahead: If you've already identified the room or spot in your house where you'd like to begin, go for it. For example, if you have company coming for dinner and you can't see your dining table under all the clutter, then it makes sense to begin there. Simply turn to the chapter that you need most and follow the Keep/Toss Checklists.

And try the ten-minute challenge: Turn the chore of decluttering into a fun challenge by setting a timer for ten minutes. Grab a bag and go to your entryway, or whichever room, closet, or drawer you decided to start in. See if you can find ten things on the toss checklist to add to the bag before the buzzer goes off. Long enough to make an impact but not so long that you lose focus, the ten-minute timer is the perfect length.

Just imagine the difference ten things can make! If you're feeling intimidated or anxious, it's only ten things. If you feel like you want to have a success, then it's a whole ten things that you've decluttered! For larger areas, it'll take multiple ten-minute sessions to finish, but consistently working in short increments adds up to real progress toward your goal.

For most of us, doing a big clean-out of that messy room that's been bugging you just overcomplicates the simple step of just doing one thing to get the ball rolling. Don't trip yourself up. Start small, see success, and then take the next step. Just start where you are and do what you can. Plus, it can be a clever way to get other people in your house involved, especially if you have kids. Make it a game, and you might even have fun decluttering.

You'll feel hopeful and organized without second-guessing yourself or feeling guilt and regret about your choices. I tell you. I help you decide. I give you clues. Together we'll keep and toss and, as a result, declutter your life. So, let the tossing begin! Turn the page and join me. I'll show you what to KEEP, what to TOSS, and why.

Create a lasting habit by tracking your progress over the next thirty days. Each day you work for ten minutes (or more), mark the chart below. At the end of thirty days, you'll have helped to create a lasting habit and have tossed out at least three hundred things!

1	2	3	4	5	6	7	8	9	10
11	12	13	14	15	16	17	18	19	20
21	22	23	24	25	26	27	28	29	30

Chapter 1

Entryway and Mudroom

With a few quick tosses, you can transform your eyesore of an entryway into an efficient space. Let's create a welcoming area you're delighted to come home to. A place you're proud to invite both expected and drop-in guests into.

The goal is to have everything you need when leaving the house easily accessible, with a spot to store the things you bring home. Between shoes, purses, shopping bags, and seven umbrellas (of which only two work), it's no wonder you're tripping over things.

Follow the checklists, paring down to what you need — and remember that what you need depends on the weather where you live, who lives in your home, and what time of year it is. To prevent the space from becoming overcrowded, store seasonal items in a less convenient location, and bring them down only when you need them.

Ask yourself these key questions:

1. Would I rather have this item or the space that it occupies in my home?
2. Would I give it away if I knew that someone else would really benefit from having this?
3. Have I been doing fine without it because I forgot I owned it?

Now, let's enter the toss zone!

Everyday Essentials

KEEP

One everyday tote, messenger bag, or briefcase that:

- can fit file folders inside (remember a standard document is 8.5" x 11")

- has pen slots and multiple compartments for organization

- closes in your preferred fashion with a zip, flap, or clasp

- offers a security feature, like a lock, if needed or required by your industry

- has a cushioned interior to protect electronics, like a laptop

- is made of a durable material that can survive daily wear and tear

- is stylish and updated enough to be used today

- is hard-sided if delicate contents will be exposed to weight or pressure

TOSS
Excess totes, messenger bags, or briefcases that:

- are excessively damaged or scuffed

- are lacking any necessary security feature

- do not offer enough protection for electronics

- are not large enough for your purposes

- are too large and cumbersome to carry

- are hopelessly out of style

- are simply too heavy to fill and use

KEEP
One purse that:

- has outside pockets for your often-reached-for items

- is lightweight

- has wide straps for better comfort

TOSS
Excess purses that:

- are oversized, which often get overfilled and heavy

- have long shoulder straps, which tend to force you to lean to one side

- are wide-bottomed, which force your elbow to stick out unnaturally

Did you know?

Many chiropractors recommend that both children and adults carry no more than 10 percent of their body weight in a bag or backpack.

STORAGE SOLUTION

Consider adopting a "pouch system," where you group and store similar items in smaller pouches, like makeup bags or even see-through zip-top bags. This allows you to easily move what you need—and only what you need—between bags.

BACKPACK RECOMMENDED SIZE CHART

If you are	Your backpack should be
36–42" tall	11" tall x 4" deep
43–47" tall	15" tall x 6" deep
4' or taller	17" tall x 7" deep

If you need to use a backpack larger than what's recommended here, you should go for one with wheels.

KEEP

For each household member who uses one, one backpack that:

- is made from extremely lightweight material, such as nylon or canvas

- has a durable, working zipper

- is water resistant, in case of a light rain or snowfall

- has a waterproof lining, which makes it easy to wipe spills clean

- has curved, padded, adjustable straps for carrying over the shoulder

- has sternum and waist straps that clip together for even weight distribution

- has a top handle for hanging from a hook

- has multiple interior pockets for organization and exterior pockets to hold commonly used items

TOSS

Backpacks that:

- have your child's full name printed on it (for safety reasons, you don't want a stranger to know your child's name, but initials are fine)

- have broken zippers, handles, or wheels

- are unstable and tip over when left unattended

- are heavy when empty, making them too heavy to carry when full

KEEP

These items in your wallet:

- Emergency notification information

- ID

- Insurance cards and information

- Two credit cards for everyday expenses

- Just enough cash for daily expenses

TOSS

These items from your wallet that you don't need or don't want someone else to get if your wallet is lost or stolen:

- Blank checks

- Medicare card

- PIN number and passwords for the cards in your wallet

- Social Security card

- Spare key

- Original photographs

- Old receipts, business cards, or notes you no longer need

KEEP

These items in your purse, briefcase, or backpack:

- Wallet

- Small key chain with keys

- Individually packaged handwipes

- Tissues

- Medication

- Bandages

- Feminine products

- Travel-size or multipurpose grooming products such as moisturizer, deodorant, hairbrush

- Hair ties (if you or your kids have long hair)

- Gum or mint, floss, and/or single-use toothbrush

- Pen

- Small notepad

- Sunglasses with case

- Makeup bag with lipstick, nail file, powder, etc.

- Two postage stamps

- Business cards

- Coupons you may want to use

- Loose change

- Multiple pens and markers (especially if they leak or don't write)

- Old receipts and lists

- Outdated appointment cards

- Oversize notebook

- Passport

- Passwords

- Store, loyalty, and membership cards (store them in the Stocard or Keyring app instead)

TOSS
These items from your purse, briefcase, or backpack:

- Business cards you no longer need

- Checkbook

- Crumbs, lint, debris, wrappers, trash

- Expired coupons

- Full makeup kit

- Gift cards (store them in the Gyft app instead)

KEEP

Multiple sizes and styles of reusable bags that:

- have a flat bottom

- can stand up themselves, making them easy to pack up and load into your car

- have a decent handle length in case you want to carry them over your shoulder

- have durable, secure seams and a well-constructed handle

- are machine washable or are made of a water-resistant material that can easily be wiped down/disinfected

- are the right size for what you carry most often

- have exterior pockets for storing little items

Make sure you include these types of reusable bags:

- 10 grocery-size

- 6 smaller, lunch-size

- 3 that are compact and lightweight and that fold to a small pouch about 3" x 5" (but open to about 18" x 18")

- 2 that are insulated to keep items either hot or cold, such as ice cream or a hot rotisserie chicken

TOSS

Excess quantities of reusable bags that:

- have broken snaps or handles that are tearing or straining at the seams

- are too dirty or contaminated to safely be reused

- are unusual sizes: gigantic totes are often too heavy to carry when full; tiny shopping bags barely hold anything

- are cheap give-away bags you got for free

- have a lingering chemical smell even after washing

- are too cumbersome, like a bag that folds in on itself or is too narrow at the top to be practical

KEEP

One lunch box or lunch tote per family member that:

- is stain-resistant

- won't leak or spill, even if the contents inside do

- has a roomy outer pocket for carrying extras, like silverware or snacks

- closes securely to prevent items from falling out

- has a wide opening, making it easy to fill and unpack

- is the right size for most meals—too small and foods won't fit; too large and foods will move around

TOSS

Lunch boxes and lunch totes that:

- can no longer be cleaned well enough to be presentable or food-safe

- are odd-shaped sizes that are not practical to use

- have designs that no longer appeal or embellishments that can easily snag on things

- are peeling or separating at the seams

- are too small to allow an ice pack or water bottle to fit if you need one

Did you know?

ChicoBag Company accepts any and all reusable bags for their recycling program. Simply mail them to: ChicoBag Company c/o Zero Waste Program, 747 Fortress Street, Chico, CA 95973. Learn more at ChicoBag.com.

In Your Over-the-Door Organizer

KEEP

These items that you need most often when going out or that need a dedicated storage spot for when you return home:

- mail to go out

- sunglasses

- electronics cords and chargers for the car

- in-season items, like sunscreen or winter gloves

- loose change

If you are a pet owner, keep:

- lint roller to de-fuzz or roll pet hair off your clothing

- one leash and harness or collar for each pet that goes outdoors

- treats

- paw wipes or a towel for rainy, muddy days

- waste disposal bags

- jackets, sweaters, bandanas (if your pet enjoys or requires being dressed up)

TOSS

These items that you no longer need everyday access to:

- out-of-season items, like sunscreen or winter gloves

- electronics cords and chargers for electronics you no longer use or own

- large amounts of loose change that can be cashed in at the bank

16 Clever Ways to Repurpose an Over-the-Door Shoe Organizer

Gain storage space by using a shoe organizer in different ways in different rooms.

1. Attic
small holiday decorations

2. Bathroom door
hair accessories, brushes, and makeup

3. Camper or RV bathroom
shampoo, body wash, shaving cream, and other personal products

4. Clothes closet
ties, socks, belts, and accessories

5. Craft room
jewelry pliers, scrapbook embellishments, knitting needles, or other craft supplies

6. Entryway
employee ID, mail to go out, sunglasses, earbuds, chargers and cords

7. Garage
air pump attachments, safety glasses, and other small items

8. Garden
hand tools, gloves, and seed packets (or use it as a hanging garden

9. Guest bedroom
bows, ribbons, and other gift wrap

10. Playroom
dolls, action figures, and other small toys

11. Kid's room
pencils, rulers, and other homework supplies

12. Laundry room
stain removers, clothes de-fuzzer, and cleaning supplies

13. Mudroom
dog leash, pet brush, travel bowl, and other pet supplies

14. Living room
CDs, DVD, remotes, and gaming controllers

15. Pantry
spice jars and packets

16. Workshop
instruction manuals, screws, nails, and small tools

Outdoor Gear

KEEP

One umbrella per household member, plus two spares, that:

- are size-appropriate for the person who needs to carry it

- are made of quick-drying fabric, allowing you to fold up and put away a dry umbrella sooner with fewer puddles on your floor

- are brightly colored so you can be seen while walking in the rain

- have a rubberized grip or ergonomic handle

- have a wrist strap so you can easily carry it when closed

TOSS

Extra umbrellas that:

- have a broken automatic-open button

- are difficult to collapse one-handed, leaving you to struggle in a downpour

- are torn, stained, have bent ribs, or smell musty or mildewed

- are missing the closure strap

- are oversized and challenging to control in strong wind or difficult to walk without poking others

- flip inside out in a strong wind because they don't have a vented canopy or a tiered or two-layer fabric construction

KEEP/TOSS CLUE: Umbrellas with deep domes provide extra coverage for your hair; compact ones are easy to toss in a tote or briefcase. But the most common is the umbrella with a canopy of fourteen inches or longer (measured when the umbrella is fully extended from the top of the rib where it meets the pole to the bottom of the rib arm). Fourteen-inch canopies are large enough to keep you dry in downpours while still being user-friendly.

KEEP
Coats, jackets, and other outerwear that:

- are comfortable to wear

- slip on and off easily

- don't get fuzz or lint on your outfit

- are flattering styles, colors, or designs

- have zippers, buttons, or closures that function properly

TOSS
Coats, jackets, or outerwear that:

- no longer fit anyone in the house

- are ripped, torn, or completely worn out

- did not get worn last season

- don't work for the season they are designed for (such as a raincoat that is not waterproof or a winter coat that does not adequately protect from cold)

KEEP
A single rain hat that:

- is waterproof (you'd be surprised!)

- is a neutral color to coordinate with almost any outfit

- has a hat brim of 3", which offers the most protection from the elements

TOSS
Rain hats that:

- take too long to dry

- are not vented (these get hot and uncomfortable to wear)

- are not a flattering shape or style

KEEP

Two sun hats/visors that:

- have an angled brim for longer, all-day protection as the sun rises and sets

- are comfortable to wear

- are made of a light-colored material (the darker the color, the more heat it absorbs)

- are in a versatile style that matches a wide variety of outfits

- have a sweatband to keep sweat from dripping down your forehead

TOSS

Sun hats/visors that:

- have less than a 3" brim, offering little sun protection

- have no hook-and-loop closure or neck cinch to prevent the hat from blowing off your head

- are hot to wear because the fabric is not vented

- have faded from the sun

KEEP
Sunglasses that:

- wrap around to protect your delicate eye area from wrinkle-causing sun damage

- include UV protection

- are flattering on your face

- are in your current prescription (if you wear prescription lenses)

- fit over your eyeglasses (if you prefer to wear this way)

- are tinted darkly enough to protect your eyes

TOSS
Sunglasses that:

- are scratched or have missing or cracked lenses

- have damaged or missing legs

- have bent frames

- are missing pieces like nose pads

- are not your current prescription

- are too small

- you don't like to wear

- are not a dark enough tint to protect your eyes in bright sun

- have a protective lens coating that is flaking off

- are left over from an eye procedure

KEEP

Baseball caps that:

- have logos you are comfortable wearing (in other words, if you're not a fan of a particular team, don't keep a baseball cap for them!)

- have adjustable straps

- fit properly

- keep you cool and the sun out of your eyes

KEEP/TOSS CLUE: Answer these two questions:

- How many people in your household wear caps in an average week? (Be sure to include anyone who wears a hat as part of a work uniform.)

- During an average week, how many days do they wear a cap?

Multiply those two numbers to get the number of caps you should keep.

TOSS

Baseball caps that:

- have no sweatband

- are tattered and torn or have appliqué that is falling off

- don't fit anyone in the house

STORAGE SOLUTION

Caps can become misshaped when hung, even on a cap rack. Store caps the same way they are displayed in stores, with the back of the cap pushed forward and stacked neatly in a box or basket.

KEEP/TOSS CLUE: If a cap is not worn but is a souvenir and holds sentimental value, keep it. But free up valuable space in the entryway by moving it to another area of your home. A cap for a favorite sports team might look nice displayed on a shelf in a home office, in a clear box on a shelf in a work area, or on a media center area in a den.

KEEP
These winter hats/ headgear (five per person):

- 2 that go with your everyday jacket

- 1 that works with your fancy coat

- 2 suited for outdoor activities (when you might be outdoors longer), like sledding or snow shoveling

Make sure the ones you keep:

- are tight enough to stay put but not so tight that they give you a headache

- are easy to slip on and off

- are easy to hold on to once you take it off, like a hat you can stuff in your pocket

- don't flatten and ruin your hairstyle

- are warm

- work in multiple ways, like a hat that includes earflaps so you can skip additional earmuffs

If you rarely wear hats for whatever reason, keep these items that are insulated to protect against cold temperatures and the wind:

- adjustable earmuffs

- ear cuffs that slip over the ears

- fleece headbands that stretch for easy on and off

TOSS
Winter hats/headgear that:

- itch or are otherwise uncomfortable to wear

- are too tight or too loose and can fall off

- have holes or ripped seams not able or worthwhile to repair

- are outgrown in size or style, like a character hat or an outlandish color or style you won't wear

- give your hair static

- do not keep you warm

- keep getting caught on your jacket collar

- attract lint and need to be cleaned often

- are too bulky to be stylish, flattering, or comfortable

- came with a jacket you no longer wear and does not coordinate with other outerwear

KEEP

Two pairs (per household member) of everyday winter gloves that:

- are machine washable

- keep your hands warm

- are made of a thin, light, quick-drying or wicking material, like spandex or polyester

- have cuffs that are long enough to tuck into your jacket sleeve for the most protection

- are a color and style that complement your everyday winter coat, hat, and scarf

TOSS

Everyday winter gloves that:

- are too tight or too loose (so that they slip off)

- have coarse stitching or manufacturer tags that irritate your skin and cannot easily be removed

- are slippery (so you can't easily grip your car's steering wheel for safe driving or anything else you may be carrying)

KEEP/TOSS CLUE: Keep a pair of dressy winter gloves for more formal occasions. Make sure they are easy-on and easy-off and don't catch on jewelry or watches.

KEEP

Two pairs of active winter gloves (for outdoor chores, like shoveling snow) that are:

- water repellent

- lined with moisture-wicking material to keep fingers dry

- washable or have a washing machine–safe removable lining

- PVC-dotted on the palm for a sturdy grip, even in freezing conditions

---

Did you know?

Knit acrylic gloves come in a variety of colors and patterns and are generally very budget-friendly. They are great for both kids and grown-ups who have a tendency to lose gloves or as a backup pair of gloves to keep in your car for emergencies.

TOSS

Active winter gloves that:

- have tearing seams

- get wet inside

- do not offer enough cushioning to be comfortable

KEEP

Three winter scarves per member of your household:

- one for every day that works with your go-to winter jacket

- one that works with your fancier winter coat

- one made of a sturdy material for prolonged outdoor activities, like snow shoveling

Make sure the ones you keep:

- match or coordinate with your hat and gloves

- don't have long fibers sticking up that can scratch your neck, blow in your face, or get stuck on lip gloss

- are made of a soft and comfortable fabric

- have a dense weave without wide gaps in the knit (lacier patterns can catch on your coat zipper or other objects)

- are wide enough to fully cover the back of your neck in order to keep the chill off

- are shorter than your everyday coat

- are machine washable

- don't get tangled in your hair

- are a color, style, and pattern that suit your current fashion sense

Winter scarves that:

- are itchy or irritating to your skin

- shed all over your clothing

- are stretched out of shape

- are missing fringe

- are fraying or unraveling

- are part of a set, such as those that come attached to a jacket you don't wear

STORAGE SOLUTION

Consider keeping one full set of winter accessories (hat, gloves, and scarf) per person in the car for the unexpected storm or the cold day when you just forgot to grab them on your way out the door.

Chapter 2

Bathrooms and Cosmetics

Have you ever wondered where all that stuff in your bathroom drawers and shelves came from? I bet you don't remember when you bought most of it or if you even remember buying it at all! Or maybe you bought it, loved it, and then bought more just in case it were to be discontinued. Now there is no way you can use all the products before it expires or goes bad.

It can be intimidating to think about tackling shelves and drawers overrun with bottles and brushes, not to mention that dark space under the bathroom sink, where who knows what is lurking. But you can declutter even this space, one toss at a time.

Remember to customize the lists to your personal style. If you lean more toward homeopathic and holistic remedies, then substitute your version of the items listed. Too much of a good thing, natural or not, is clutter. If you just don't use that much makeup, feel free to toss all your cosmetics brushes.

Ask yourself these key questions:
1. Is it expired, questionable, or past its useable prime?
2. Is it irritating, the wrong color, an offensive scent, or otherwise unusable?
3. Is it something I no longer use because I've changed my style?

Let's check inside the cabinet, pull open the vanity drawers, and—finally—look under the sink.

Body Care

KEEP

No more than two toothbrushes per person in your household that:

- have your preferred bristle firmness

- have a small enough head for easy maneuvering around your teeth

- are less than four months old (once in use, and three years if still unopened)

TOSS

Toothbrushes that:

- are rechargeable or electric but that no longer function

- have bent or worn bristles

- were in a travel container and unable to completely dry (which breeds bacteria)

KEEP

Razors that:

- still give a close shave

- you can get a good grip on, even when wet

- feature a pivoting head with great control

- get the job done in one pass

TOSS

Razors that have:

- dull, rusty, or gunked-up blades

- broken handles

- a worn-off moisture strip

- give you razor burn

KEEP
Shaving lotion/aftershaves that:

- come in your preferred formulation, like cream versus gel

- work for a closer, smoother, less irritating shave

- are for a specific area of skin, like face versus legs

- feel refreshing and smell great

TOSS
Shaving lotion/aftershaves that:

- irritate your skin

- have a fragrance you don't like

- clog your razor

- burn on application

KEEP
Soap/body washes that:

- have a nice scent

- leave your skin feeling clean but don't dry it out

TOSS
Soap/body washes that:

- have changed consistency or color

- are older than a year and contain essential oils or milk

KEEP
Body sponges that still:

- lather well

- dry quickly, preventing bacteria

- offer gentle exfoliation without being harsh

TOSS
Body sponges that are:

- mesh and have been in use for eight weeks or longer

- loofahs and have been in use four weeks or longer

- discolored or ragged

KEEP

Deodorant that:

- works to keep you dry and smelling fresh

- is the application you prefer (solid, gel, roll-on) and goes on smoothly

- is long-lasting

- does not stain or damage your clothing

- doesn't ball up on your underarm

TOSS

Deodorant that:

- has a broken dispenser

- is dried out or crumbly

- is one year or older

- has a fragrance that has changed

- keeps falling out of the container

KEEP

Fragrances that:

- you really like

- don't stain your clothing

- you wear daily or is your "go-to" scent, or is your preferred evening scent if you like to switch it up

TOSS

Fragrances that:

- smell different than when you bought it

- you no longer like

- are discolored

- give you a headache when you wear it

- wear off too easily to be useful

- came as part of a gift set you never opened or used

Did you know?

You can switch out harsh, scratchy sponges and nylon poofs for baby washcloths. Not only do they gently exfoliate the skin, but baby washcloths can also easily be washed, so you won't need to replace them as often.

Skin Care and Antiaging Products

KEEP

Moisturizers that are:

- noncomedogenic and less likely to clog pores

- a light and good-for-daytime version with SPF 15+

- a thicker, richer nighttime formula without SPF

TOSS

Moisturizers that:

- have a scent you do not like

- cause breakouts

- are wrong for your current skin type or problem areas

KEEP

Facial cleansers that are:

- mild but effective

- a milky or cream version if you have dry skin

- a gel formulation if you have an oily complexion

- pulling double duty as a makeup remover

TOSS

Facial cleansers that:

- have irritating fragrances or dyes

- do not remove oil and dirt well

- leave your face feeling tight and dry

KEEP

Makeup removers that:

- remove all makeup, even waterproof mascara

- are easy to grab and use, like wipes

- won't clog pores, sting, irritate or dry out your skin or eyes, or leave a residue

TOSS

Makeup removers that are:

- irritating to your skin, possibly because of fragrances or dyes

- unnecessary because your facial cleaner also removes makeup

KEEP

These three bottles of sunscreen:

- a lightweight, noncomedogenic formula for your face that's good for daily use (at least SPF 15)

- a waterproof and/or sweat-resistant formula for swimming and outdoor activities, like yardwork (at least SPF 30)

- a spray- or pump-based bottle of lotion that you can easily toss in your bag and is safe for all over your face and body (at least SPF 30)

TOSS

Sunscreen that:

- is past the average three-year expiration date (check the package; some expire much sooner)

- has been exposed to high temperatures for a few days, like in a hot car or a beach bag for a few days

---

Did you know?

Most manufacturers recommend storing your sunscreen around 75 degrees, but a hot car or a tote bag left in the sun can reach 100-plus degrees. That extreme heat can break down the all-important UV-absorbing chemicals, making the product much less effective. Carrying sunscreen in a cooler bag, especially during the hot months, can help it last longer.

KEEP
Exfoliators that:

- gently do the job without being rough on your skin

- use natural fruit enzymes for added moisture

- have a nonirritating fragrance

TOSS
Exfoliators that are:

- overly coarse or abrasive

- too fine to be effective

- irritating to your skin

KEEP
Serums that are:

- concentrated specifically for your problem area, like brightening, acne, or antiaging

- fragrance-free or a nonirritating fragrance

TOSS
Serums that are:

- irritating to your skin

- for skin problems you no longer have or never had

- older than one year

KEEP
Eye creams that include:

- skin-tightening caffeine

TOSS
Eye creams that are:

- irritating to your sensitive eye area

- ineffective

- older than one year

KEEP

Antiaging/beauty creams and gadgets that:

- you actually use on a regular basis (i.e., once per week at minimum)

- are three months old or newer (for creams only)

TOSS

Antiaging/beauty creams and gadgets that:

- show any separation in product

- show changes in the color or consistency

- you never take the time to use

- you have more than one of or that treat the same problem as something else you like and use regularly

KEEP

Foot creams that:

- are formulated to penetrate the extra-thick skin on the foot

- actually work to relieve dry skin

- smell pleasant to you

TOSS

Foot creams that:

- don't absorb well

- have an offensive fragrance

- you never use

- include ingredients you don't need, like an antifungal

KEEP

Foot smoothers that:

- work to remove dry skin and calluses

- are easy to use

- are simple to clean

TOSS

Foot smoothers that:

- no longer work as intended

- are so coarse they hurt your feet

- cut your skin

- don't work well due to a dulled blade or worn grit

Spa Products

KEEP

Facial muds, masks, peels, and waxes that:

- treat a skin problem you currently have

- don't irritate your skin

- actually do what they claim

- you use at least once per month

TOSS

Facial muds, masks, peels, and waxes that:

- are too time-consuming to use

- you prefer to get done at the spa or salon

- have a scent you dislike

- leave your skin feeling tight, dry, or irritated

- you keep saving for a self-pampering weekend that never happens

KEEP

Spa products and machines that:

- work well and are easy to operate

- you have the space to store

- you actually use at least monthly

TOSS

Spa products and machines you never or rarely use, such as:

- aloe-infused gloves and socks

- bubble baths or bath salts that sit around looking pretty

- essential oils older than one year (after that, the chemistry of the oils can change)

- unopened gift sets and spa kits that never made it out of the box

- tub bubbler that is too difficult to set up for just one bath

Hair Care

KEEP

Hair-care and styling products that:

- actually work for your hair

- you use regularly

- have a nice fragrance

TOSS

These hair-care and styling products:

- barely used bottles you tried only once

- bottles that leak or have broken dispensers

- shampoo, conditioners, gels, and other products three years or older

KEEP

Brushes and combs that:

- are gentle and don't damage your hair

- have a round shape if you need volume

- have a comfortable grip

- are easy to clean

TOSS

Brushes and combs that:

- are broken or are missing bristles

- hurt your scalp

- you forgot you even own

KEEP

Hair-styling tools that:

- work with your hair as it is now

- are your go-to style tools

- are gentle on your hair, such as velvet-covered hot rollers

- have an automatic "off" feature for safety

TOSS

Hair-styling tools that:

- are missing parts

- don't coordinate or work together, like a diffuser that does not fit your hair dryer

- burn, break, or damage your hair

- have a damaged cord

- do not function properly or have difficult-to-read controls

KEEP/TOSS CLUE: Men can accumulate just as many grooming products as women. Toss products that don't work as advertised, like hair-loss solutions or razors that leave patches of hair. And toss the items you don't need, like guide combs or blade oil for hair clippers you no longer own. But keep the go-to microtrimmer for nose and ear hair and the fresh styptic pencil, as well as the electric hair/beard trimmer if you actually use it for touch-ups between salon appointments.

Nail Care

KEEP
Nail clippers that:

- are easy to grasp

- clip easily without tugging or tearing the nail

- have a nail catcher to trap clippings for easy disposal

- are wide enough in the jaw to cut even a thick nail

If you are a parent:

- baby nail clippers that are in good shape and don't slip while cutting

TOSS
Nail clippers that:

- are inaccurate or don't have a guard, which means you can clip too low

- leave a rough edge

KEEP/TOSS CLUE: Chances are, you don't need all the manicure tools that come in a nail set. Keep the ones that work well and toss the rest.

Did you know?

Nail polish is considered a hazardous waste because it is flammable and contains toxic chemicals. Instead of throwing it in the trash, call the National Recycling Hotline at 800-CLEANUP, log onto Earth911.com, or bring it to your next local hazardous waste collection date in town.

KEEP

These nail polishes:

- 1 neutral shade good for everyday wear (doesn't need a touch-up as often because it doesn't show chips)

- 1 trendy color just for fun or for your toes in a professional environment

- 4 seasonal colors to coordinate with your outfits

- 1 clear top coat, which keeps your nail color looking good longer

- 1 ridge-filling base coat for a smooth color application

KEEP/TOSS CLUE: If you never touch up at home and always go to the salon, just toss all your polishes. However, bringing your own color with you means you can touch up at home without an additional trip to the salon.

TOSS

These nail polishes:

- unflattering colors for your skin tone

- uber-trendy colors that you no longer love

- colors that are unwearable in the workplace

- formulas that turn your nails yellow or otherwise damage your nails

- those that are difficult to apply (too thick or leave globs) or to remove

- those with damaged brushes or bristles that leave nails streaky

- leaky or broken bottles that you can't open or close properly

- mostly empty bottles you keep hoping you can get more out of

- any formulation that has changed consistency or color

Cosmetics

KEEP
These items for your face:

- concealer with the creamiest formula that works with your skin tone for covering under-eye circles and blemishes

- foundation or tinted moisturizer, depending on the level of coverage you prefer

- translucent powder to set your makeup and control shine

TOSS
Face makeup that:

- is older than one year or shows a change in consistency

- isn't the right color for your skin tone

- looks cakey or obvious when you wear it

KEEP/TOSS CLUE: Your coverage level and color choices for face makeup may change with the seasons. Since most products expire within 12 months or less, buy the travel size versions to use without the waste.

KEEP
These products for your eyes:

- 1 mascara that you like, doesn't clump, and does not irritate your eyes

- 1 buildable mascara where you can wear one coat for daytime and add a layer or two for a night out (maybe that even curls your lashes)

- 1 eye shadow palette with neutral shades, like beige or taupe (instant eye brighteners that are basically goof-proof and universally flattering)

- 1 eye shadow palette that offers a variety of finishes, like matte and a shimmery highlight shade to complete daytime and evening looks

- 2 eye pencils in neutrals that work best with your eye color

- 1 fun "night out" liner to play with your eye color in a nonprofessional environment

KEEP/TOSS CLUE: Keep the liner that brings out your eye color. Black eyeliner is a standard go-to, but you might find a new favorite liner to keep. Try:

- Dark green liner if you have brown eyes
- Gold liner if you have amber eyes
- Copper liner if you have blue eyes
- Navy blue liner if you have gray eyes
- Plum liner if you have green eyes
- Bronze liner if you have hazel eyes

TOSS
These eye products:

- eye shadow primer (it's unnecessary if you use a deeply pigmented, non-creasing shadow)

- mascara more than three months old

- liquid eyeliner over three months old, to lessen your risk of eye irritation

KEEP
These cheek makeup products:

- a flattering blush and bronzer duo (the best way to choose a blush color is to lightly pinch your cheek and pick a blush shade that most closely resembles your natural flush)

- a blush with multiple colors in one brick that allows you to customize your look without needing multiple compacts

- a highlighter shade to apply above the cheek bone, in the corner of your eye near your nose, or under your eyebrow to make you look more awake

TOSS

These cheek makeup products:

- blush with large pieces of glitter that looks too young for you

- anything in a color that is too bright or unnatural-looking

- anything that clogs your pores or causes a reaction on your skin

- anything in a formulation (liquid, mousse, gel, powder, cream) you don't like

KEEP

These lipsticks, glosses, and liners:

- 2 lipsticks—one for a daytime look and one for an evening out

- 5 lip glosses in a variety of shades that can be worn alone or on top of lipsticks to create new looks

- 1 lip liner that is about one shade darker than your natural lip color (this gives you fuller-looking lips)

TOSS

These lip products:

- lipsticks and lip glosses that are one year old or older and lip pencils that are three years or older

- anything that has a funny taste or smell

- any lipstick or lip gloss that has turned cakey or gummy or does not go on smoothly

- broken tubes of lipstick or broken pots of gloss (unless you have a replacement container on hand and will transfer the item immediately)

- any lip product that irritates your lips

KEEP/TOSS CLUE: To prevent reactions and blemishes, toss expired makeup and makeup that hasn't been cared for properly, like a sponge that was left moist in a powder compact.

KEEP

These five makeup brushes:

- foundation brush: flat, firm, non-streaking, nonshedding

- blush/powder brush: medium-sized, soft to slightly firm, slightly angled

- small round brush: soft, for use in eye creases

- brow and eyeliner brushes: firmly bristled with a slanted tip

- blending brush: large, soft, easy to clean, and quick drying

TOSS

These unnecessary makeup brushes:

- large fan face brush
- large powder brush
- contour powder brush
- blending eye brush
- large eye shadow brush
- medium eye shadow brush
- foam or sponge eye-crease brush
- concealer brush
- lip brush
- fine eye- or lip-liner brush
- compact lip brush
- fluffy powder brush

Did you know?

Most makeup brushes should be cleaned weekly. Once a brush loses its shape, sheds, or frays, it should be discarded.

KEEP

These beauty gadgets:

- one eyelash curler that works without pulling or pinching

- one eyebrow comb

TOSS

These beauty gadgets:

- unnecessary eyelash curlers, if your mascara has curling properties

- eyelash curlers that pinch your eyelid or break your delicate lashes, and heated eyelash curlers that do not work

- brow trimmers that are difficult to maneuver and could take off too much hair

- eyelash combs that gunk up quickly, do not clean easily, or are painful to use because they have sharp or very pointed teeth

- the eyebrow comb, if you prefer to simply use a toothbrush (dedicated for makeup use only)

- unnecessary eyelash combs, if your mascara is extra defining

KEEP

Tweezers that:

- have a nonslip grip and a slant tip for precision

- have a magnifying glass attached (especially useful when removing splinters)

- are stainless steel, because they are long-lasting, easy to clean, and won't rust

TOSS

Tweezers that:

- are too sharp in the tip, making them painful to use

- do not grasp well

- aren't well aligned, resulting in missing hairs when tweezing

- aren't very precise and tend to pinch your skin

First Aid and Medication

KEEP

Any items that:

- are prescription and you are currently taking or using

- are nonprescription and still good

- are for temporary conditions for which you would conceivably use them again within the next two to three years, such as a wrist brace or an elasticized cloth bandage

TOSS

Any items that:

- are expired (this includes eye drops and nasal sprays)

- are discolored, dried out, separated, or in any way different than when you first purchased them

- are prescriptions for an ailment or condition from which you no longer suffer (remove any labels with personal information before tossing the bottles)

Did you know?

You should never toss expired or unneeded drugs in the garbage, where children or pets or others may be able to get them. Nor should you flush medications down the toilet; it can cause water contamination. Instead, dispose of medications (including EpiPens and asthma inhalers) by bringing them to your local pharmacy or turning them in at a community prescription take-back program or hazardous waste cleanup day. Check TakeBackDay.dea.gov to find out where to find collection boxes near you. Some police stations also have a secure drop box.

KEEP

These medical supplies:

- custom-made orthotics

- canes for different walking surfaces, with a rubberized tip or tripod

- cane or walker that is the proper height and is still used or might be needed in the near future

---

31 First-Aid Items to Keep

1. A list of emergency numbers, including the poison control center, doctors, and a trusted neighbor
2. Address of your local hospital
3. Acetaminophen
4. Adhesive bandages in a variety of sizes
5. Aloe vera gel
6. Antacids
7. Antibiotic ointment
8. Antidiarrheal treatment
9. Athlete's foot cream

10. Antihistamines
11. Any prescription medications currently taken by family members
12. Burn ointment
13. Calamine lotion
14. Cough medicine
15. Decongestant
16. Disposable gloves
17. Epsom salt
18. Eyedrops
19. Eye wash solution
20. Gauze bandages and pads

21. Heating pad for sore muscles
22. Hydrocortisone cream
23. Hydrogen peroxide
24. Ibuprofen
25. Ice pack
26. Insect sting ointment
27. Laxatives
28. Scissors
29. Thermometer
30. Throat lozenges
31. Tweezers with angled tips, which are best for splinters

TOSS

These medical supplies:

- orthotics that are broken or torn, or if any plastic is cracked

- orthotics that are one year or older and need to be adjusted

- old splints, braces, or walking boots that are meant for one-time use

- commode or urinal that is no longer needed and won't be needed in the near future

- wheelchair or crutches that are no longer needed

Must-Have Medical Supplies for Kids

- Child-safe insect repellent

- Child-safe sunscreen

- Infant and/or child thermometers (both digital and ear or rectal)

- Rehydration fluids for children with tummy trouble

- Children's and/or infants' acetaminophen and ibuprofen, as recommended by your doctor, to relieve fever and mild pain

- Phone numbers for your pediatrician or emergency contacts

- The American Association of Poison Control Centers' website (poison.org) or national emergency hotline (800-222-1222)

Chapter 3
Closets and Laundry Area

Should your closets be secured shut with caution tape because you risk items toppling down when you open the doors? Closets are the most popular choices for tucking items so they are out of sight. Problem is, if you rarely sort through what you've shoved inside, the space gets cluttered quickly.

It can be challenging to figure out storage solutions for the unsightly plunger, rolls of unruly gift wrap, and loads of laundry . . . especially when not all laundering areas are created equal. You may have a dedicated laundry room, a stacked washer and dryer in a nook, or you may tote your laundry out to a Laundromat or your building's laundry room. Regardless of the space you have—or don't have—you still have laundry and clothing-care supplies, and you might not need to keep them all.

Ask yourself these key questions:
1. If I keep it, will I remember I have it? If I remember I have it, will I be able to find it?
2. Have I (or anyone else in my home) used this item in the last year?
3. Is keeping this item getting in the way of my ability to find what I really need when I need it?

Let's open the closet doors and drawers, shine a light on all the clutter you've been keeping, and decide what you need to keep and what should be tossed.

Laundry

KEEP
These laundry supplies:

- detergent you like and that does the job

- your preferred form of detergent (choose the pods, liquid, or powder)

- stain-lifting detergent in case you have clothes with serious stains, like grass

- HE detergent if you have a high-efficiency washing machine

- stain removers and pretreaters that remove your most common stains

- static-reducing dryer balls so you can skip dryer sheets

- color-grabbing sheets in case you wash a mixed load of laundry (lights and darks), so that colors don't bleed and redeposit on other pieces

TOSS
Laundry supplies that:

- are duplicates (if you use an all-in-one detergent, you can toss the single items it replaces)

- are samples that you will never try

- are designed for standard washing machines if you own an HE washer

- are fragrance-laden detergents if you have sensitive skin

- don't get clothes clean

- are empty or expired (chlorine bleach, for instance, has a shelf life of about one year)

- are unnecessary, like fabric softeners, if you don't use or need them

- leave residue or marks on clothes

White distilled vinegar and baking soda are chemical-free, inexpensive options to replace multiple laundry products. Vinegar is a fantastic fabric softener and odor remover—just add ½ cup to the final rinse. Add ½ cup of baking soda to the wash when you add your detergent to make your whites whiter and brights brighter.

KEEP

Laundry baskets and hampers that:

- include a lid to keep contents concealed

- have openings for good airflow for ventilating clothes inside

- are functional and hold all of your laundry between washes

- are well constructed, with a sturdy frame

- offer multiple compartments to presort whites and darks or to separate dry cleaning from the regular wash

- are snag-proof, if wicker

- include a machine-washable liner bag (with drawstring closure if you'll take it to the Laundromat)

- are made of a flexible plastic, making them easy to bend to fit through narrow doorways

TOSS

Laundry baskets and hampers that:

- are too small for your laundry needs

- are starting to fray

- have pieces breaking off

- have a wood lacquer or paint that is peeling

- have broken hinges

- have casters that won't roll

- scratch your floor when moved

- have joints that have loosened too much

- can't be kept in the bathroom because they are made of real wood that warps with humidity

KEEP

Laundry bags and specialty wash pods that:

- come with a drawstring closure

- are lightweight but sturdy

- keep the shape of the ball cap throughout the laundering process, like the Cap Washer

- have a mesh pod to keep delicates safe while washing

- have a delicates bag that holds the size garments you need to wash

- have a rust-resistant zipper

- include a snap to prevent the bag from opening during the wash cycle

- are for washing lingerie, knit sweaters, and loose-weave articles

- have durable carrying handles for easy transport

- have side pocket for storage of detergent bottles and stain sticks, if you take clothes to the Laundromat or your building's laundry room

TOSS

Laundry bags and specialty wash pods that:

- have handles too long to carry or too short to fit over your shoulder

- have torn handles that can't be stitched back on and still be strong

- have broken or missing drawstrings

- are not made of a mildew-resistant material

- hold too much laundry, making it too heavy to carry when full

- are pop-up bags that no longer pop up

- have torn mesh

- have dividers that are held in place with hook and loop or cheap snaps that easily come undone

- are made of material that is deteriorating, leaving flakes on freshly washed clothes

KEEP

One drying rack that:

- fits in the bathtub so you can lay out sopping wet clothes without having to clean up wet puddles on the floor

- has enough drying space to hold the clothes you need to lay out at one time

- is rust resistant

- has a flat, smooth surface (such as netting stretched across the rods) to prevent creases or damage

- has locking legs to prevent accidental collapse

- includes a strap to ensure it is securely closed when folded

TOSS

Drying racks that:

- are difficult to set up

- collapse too easily

- you don't have room to store

- have feet that aren't capped, risking damage to the surface you place it on

- aren't adjustable or can't hold a variety of garment shapes and sizes

- sag under the weight of wet clothes

KEEP

These clothes hangers:

- absorbent cedar hangers (a natural pest repellent), if moths or moisture is an issue

- tiered hangers, which allow you to hold multiple garments on the same hanger in limited space

- clamp hangers for hanging skirts and pants from their cuffs to avoid indentations or wrinkles

- notched or nonslip hangers for hanging up slippery items, like tank tops and camisoles

- belt hanger

- scarf hanger

STORAGE SOLUTION

If you need more closet room, consider slim, space-saving hangers, which are just one-third the size of standard hangers but are just as durable.

TOSS

These clothes hangers:

- hangers that bow under the weight of clothing

- broken or bent hangers

- wire hangers that leave bumps in clothes

- time-consuming styles, like flocked hangers that require you to adjust the clothes because they stick to the hanger

- oversize or bulky hangers, like wooden ones that take up too much space

- hangers that came with undergarments, like bras, that you won't use because you fold the items

- fancy, cute, or satin-padded hangers that came with a specialty garment but are not practical for day-to-day hanging

KEEP THIS, TOSS THAT

KEEP

One ironing board that:

- has a rest for the iron to prevent scorching the board

- is the correct size for the type of ironing you do (a tabletop version of about 30" x 12" for craft projects or touch-ups, and a free-standing version averaging 54" x 14" for clothing)

- includes a reflective surface, which speeds up the ironing process by reflecting the heat back onto the clothes

- offers an adjustable height to ensure a comfortable working surface, which for most people is hip height

- has a sleeve attachment (the slim board that makes ironing shirt sleeves a lot easier)

- includes a lock to prevent the table from collapsing

- has a nonstick surface to prevent clothing from sticking to the board when heated

TOSS

Ironing boards that:

- do not lock when folded to prevent it from popping open when you carry it

- have a permanent cover that is lumpy, bumpy, or torn

- are unstable, wobbly, or bent

- are installed in a fold-down cabinet but no longer fold out properly

- are too cumbersome to move to where you need it

KEEP
These sewing kit basics:

- 12 safety pins in a variety of sizes

- hem tape for needle-free repairs

- midsize needles that are of a medium thickness for most sewing projects

- 1 pair of sewing scissors

- 1 pincushion

- 1 tape measure

- 1 thimble

- 1 seam ripper

- 6 Velcro patches or iron-on strips with adhesive for temporary fixes

- 1 spool of carpet thread, which is thicker and more durable, to sew things like buttons

- thread in these colors: black, gray, navy, cream, white, denim-stitch gold

- 2 iron-on patches

- 2 needle threaders

TOSS
These sewing items:

- spools with too little thread left on them to be useful

- colors of thread that do not match anything you ever sew

- dull sewing scissors

- bent seam rippers

- needles that are either too thin or too thick for your sewing projects

- pincushions that are torn or otherwise falling apart

KEEP/TOSS CLUE: Keep a permanent marker handy to label the bag of extra thread and buttons that come attached to new clothes. That way, when you pare down the button collection, you'll know what goes with what and if you even still own it!

Cleaning Supplies

KEEP

Six large cleaning towels that:

- are made of microfiber, which clean spills, stains, scuff marks, mud, sticky messes, and pet hair without leaving lint behind

- are absorbent, so the mess is not just spread around

If you have a child under 5 years old, add:

- 2 more large cleaning towels for big messes or messy projects

If you are a pet owner, add:

- 2 bath-sized towels per pet that gets bathed

- 4 additional small rags for cleanup

TOSS

Cleaning towels that:

- are too grimy or permanently discolored

- leave a lint trail behind

- are ratty, ripped, fraying, or threadbare

- you'd be embarrassed to hand to a guest for cleanup

> **STORAGE SOLUTION**
>
> Stop wasting time folding cleaning rags; instead, hang a reusable shopping tote bag from a hook and just toss them inside after laundering them.

KEEP

Cleaning solutions that:

- actually clean well

- have a scent you like

- clean something you need to clean (if you don't have hardwood floors, toss the hardwood floor cleaner!)

TOSS

Cleaning solutions that:

- make stains worse or damage the surface you are trying to clean

- have changed in consistency

- are clumpy, lumpy, or watery

- have a noxious scent

- you won't realistically use before they get really old

---

12 Cleaning-Caddy Essentials

Make cleaning easier by storing your most commonly used tools in a small caddy or bucket that you can tote from room to room. Save space by nesting a smaller toteable bucket inside your larger cleaning bucket. Include these essentials in your caddy or bucket:

1. All-purpose household cleaner
2. Disinfecting wipes
3. Mild abrasive cleanser
4. Glass cleaner
5. Floor and furniture polish
6. Old toothbrush
7. Paper towels
8. Rubber gloves
9. Microfiber or lint-free cleaning cloths
10. Scouring pads
11. Sponge eraser
12. Sponges

KEEP THIS, TOSS THAT

It's a good idea to tape "how-to" directions and a map of the location for shutting off gas, water, and electric to the inside of your utility cabinet or laundry room door.

KEEP
One broom that:

- is angled for getting into corners

- has a dustpan that attaches to the broom handle for easy storage

- is soft and won't scratch floors

- has a rubberized handle tip to keep it from sliding when propped against a wall

- has a hanging-hole for easy storage

- has densely packed, synthetic bristles with feathered ends perfect for picking up even the smallest bit of debris

- is durable with a padded handle for comfort

TOSS
Extra brooms that:

- just kick up the dirt

- have sparse bristles that miss pet hair, potted plant soil, cereal, or broken glass

- shed, causing you more to clean up

- streak or mark the floor or ceiling

- are heavy and difficult to maneuver

Did you know?

An easy way to let wet rubber gloves dry out is to hang them from spring clips stuck on the inside of the broom cabinet door.

KEEP

A vacuum cleaner that:

- is either a canister, upright, handheld, stick, electric broom, or robotic, or a combination of two

- has a long wand for reaching all areas and includes accessories you need, like an upholstery brush or crevice tools for your vehicle

- has a headlight to see under spaces as you clean

- has a narrow footprint and a low profile for fitting in small spaces and under furniture

- has an easy-to-remove dust cap that is large enough to complete the cleaning job before having to empty

- has a high-efficiency particulate air (HEPA) filter and is certified Asthma and Allergy Friendly

- has strong suction power

- cleans stairs easily

- has a long battery life (if cordless)

- is lightweight and easy to maneuver

KEEP/TOSS CLUE: Keep one or two vacuums to cover all your cleaning needs. For example, you might need a canister vacuum on the second floor of your home to clean carpeted bedrooms, while a cordless stick vacuum might be all you need to keep downstairs for your hardwood floors.

TOSS

Vacuum cleaners or accessories that:

- no longer function properly

- go with vacuums you no longer own

- you no longer need or use

- no longer hold a charge or have a missing or broken charger that is not cost effective to replace (if cordless)

- are too heavy to handle, difficult to maneuver, or too noisy to operate

- lose suction power or are broken beyond repair

- easily overheat

- don't have washable filters and filters are costly to replace

21 Broom-Closet Essentials

1. Broom
2. Bucket
3. Mop
4. Plunger
5. Dustpan
6. Extendable handheld duster or dust mop
7. Trash can liners/trash bags
8. Recycling bags
9. Full-size canister or upright vacuum
10. Stick or handheld vacuum for small spills or touch-ups
11. Iron and/or garment steamer
12. Ironing board
13. Extension cord
14. Batteries
15. Flashlight
16. Light bulbs
17. Matches and a lighter
18. Step stool
19. Calendar for recycling and trash schedule
20. Spare set of house keys (clearly labeled)
21. Phone numbers for the professionals you call most often (plumber, electrician, electric company, gas company, alarm company, and poison control—which you hope you never have to call)

KEEP
These mops:

- 1 for quick touch-up jobs, like a mop with premoistened pads or microfiber pads and a solution dispenser

- 1 in a traditional style for deep cleaning or larger jobs

TOSS
Extra mops that:

- are tough to wring out

- have a mop head that does not fit in your bucket

- leave too much residual water on your hardwood floors

Tools and Cords

KEEP

Cords and chargers that:

- you use regularly; label them so you know what they belong to

TOSS

Cords and chargers that:

- are damaged and a hazard to use

- do not belong to anything you still own

KEEP/TOSS CLUE: If you come across an unknown cord, label it "unknown" with an expiration date of one year. One year gives you enough time to try to locate the match; for example, in eight months you might find it goes to a holiday decoration. If you find the match, relabel it; if not, toss it!

What to Keep in a Mini Toolkit

- Small hammer for easy projects, like hanging a picture hook

- Level

- Needle-nose pliers

- Box cutter

- 5' tape measure

- All-in-one screwdriver with multiple bits stored in the handle

- One tiny screwdriver for opening the battery compartments on things like a remote control

- Superglue

In Case of Emergency, Be Prepared— and Organized!

Keep these basic supplies on hand so you'll have what you need to get through emergency situations. And in case you need to leave your home, store your supplies in an easy-to-carry backpack. Depending on where you live and the emergency situations you could face—like an earthquake, hurricane, or tornado—you may want to pack more specific supplies. You can log onto FEMA.gov (the Federal Emergency Management Agency) to find additional recommendations based on your region.

KEEP

These emergency kit supplies:

- battery-powered or hand-crank radio (NOAA Weather Radio)
- blankets or sleeping bags
- bottles of commonly used over-the-counter medication, like antacids
- copies of personal documents (medication list and pertinent medical information, proof of address, deed/lease to home, passports, birth certificates, insurance policies)
- duct tape
- entertainment items (like a deck of cards or game of checkers)
- extra batteries in all sizes
- extra cash (credit card machines and ATMs may not work if the power is out)
- extra clothing, hat, and sturdy shoes per family member
- extra set of car keys and house keys
- family- and emergency-contact information
- first-aid kit
- flashlight

- 1 gallon of household liquid bleach to disinfect, if needed

- manual can opener

- map of the area

- matches and lighter

- medical supplies (hearing aids with extra batteries, syringes, etc.)

- multipurpose tool, like a Swiss army knife

- nonperishable food in easy-to-open containers (two-week supply)

- 1 spare bath towel per family member for "whatever," like cleaning, showering, padding under a makeshift bed, or extra warmth

- portable battery pack for charging devices like a cell phone or tablet when there is no power

- prescription medications (7–14 days' worth is ideal, especially for life-saving medications like epilepsy drugs; speak with your prescribing doctor to see how to do this—he or she may offer you samples—and be sure to keep track of the medications' expiration dates)

- sanitation and personal-hygiene items (including a toothbrush and deodorant)

- scissors

- spare glasses and/or contact lenses (if you wear them)

- sterile eye wash

- surgical masks

- thermal mylar emergency blanket to help you retain much more body heat than a traditional blanket

- water (one gallon per person, per day, for a two-week supply)

- whistle

- work gloves

If you have children:
- bottles or sippy cups

- formula or baby food

- diapers

- games and activities for children

If you have pets, add these emergency items, as appropriate, for your pet:

- 14 days' worth of canned (pop-top) or dry food (be sure to rotate every two months)

- a traveling bag, crate, or sturdy carrier, ideally one for each pet

- blanket

- bottled water, at least 14 days' worth for each pet

- disposable garbage bags for cleanup

- disposable litter trays (aluminum roasting pans are perfect) with scoopable litter

- extra collar or harness, as well as an extra leash

- grooming items

- liquid dish soap and disinfectant

- medications and medical records, especially vaccination records, stored in a waterproof container

- newspapers

- paper towels

- pet bowls

- recent photos of your pets (in case you are separated and need to make "lost" posters)

- toys

Put these items in a sturdy waterproof box as a first-aid kit for your pet:

- a list of phone numbers—your regular vet, the emergency vet, animal control, and animal poison-control numbers

- a muzzle

- antiseptic wash or wipes

- diphenhydramine (aka Benadryl—check with your vet for proper dosage)

- extra towels, wash cloths, and a blanket

- a large eye dropper (to flush wounds or administer fluids by mouth)

- latex gloves

- QuikClot or something similar to stop small wounds from bleeding

- gauze

- scissors

- sterile eye wash

- nail trimmer and styptic pencil

- tweezers

TOSS
Emergency kit supplies that:

- are expired

- have degraded in storage

KEEP/TOSS CLUE: Jot a reminder on your calendar for every three months to rotate the stored food and water with fresh supplies. Use the older items.

Linen Closet

KEEP

Sheet sets that:

- are for mattress sizes you actually own

- have deep pockets to fit your mattress with toppers

- match your current decor

- are wrinkle-free

- are a comfortable fabric, such as flannel for the winter and cotton for the summer

TOSS

Sheet sets that:

- are scratchy or irritating to your skin

- have shrunk in the wash and no longer fit well

- the color rubs off or bleeds in the wash

- are pilling or have threadbare spots

- tear easily or you need to tug to get it on the mattress

- pop off corners of the mattress

KEEP/TOSS CLUE: Keep two sets of sheets per bed in the house (one on the bed and one in the wash or in the closet, ready to use). And if you are a parent of a child 10 years old or younger, keep four fitted sheets per child bed for nighttime accidents or sick days when the sheets need to be changed multiple times.

STORAGE SOLUTION

Attach a few towel bars on the back of the linen closet door for even more hanging space. Make the most of the space by staggering the bars.

Hall Closet

KEEP
These six greeting cards on hand:

- birthday

- blank

- congratulations

- get well

- sympathy

- thank you

TOSS
Greeting cards that:

- are faded or have bent edges

- have envelopes that have lost their adhesiveness

- don't have matching envelopes

- were sent from charities requesting a donation, if you do not feel a connection to the charity, don't like the design or quality of the card, or have so many you could not possibly mail them all in a lifetime

KEEP/TOSS CLUE: Only keep cards for unexpected events, like a sympathy card, or for spur-of-the-moment sentiments, like a thank you. Other cards are best picked up when you receive the invitations, like for a baby shower or for common holidays, like Father's Day. Otherwise, over time they may get damaged; you'll forget you have them or where you put them; or you'll prefer something you saw in the store.

KEEP

These items for wrapping gifts:

- pen (colorful or metallic) for addressing cards

- ribbon, curling (three spools in coordinating colors)

- scissors

- tape—regular and double-sided

- tissue paper (three coordinating colors—one white and two others of your choice)

- 8 gift bags (one extra small, two small, two medium, two large, one extra-large)

- 3 rolls of gift wrap: one white, which works for almost any occasion; one fun and fanciful print; and one solid color of your choice.

TOSS

These gift-wrapping supplies:

- gift bags that have been written on

- ripped, crumpled, faded, or torn wrapping paper

- bows with worn-out adhesive

Did you know?

You can keep an open roll of gift wrap from unraveling by making a "cuff" from the cardboard tube inside a roll of paper towels. Simply cut it lengthwise and then snap it around the roll of wrap to keep it closed.

Pet Supplies

KEEP

These treats and feeding supplies, depending on your type of pet:

- food dish that is in good condition and easy to wash

- water bottles and dispensers that are easy for your pet to drink from

- water bowl or dispenser that is easy to disinfect as needed

- food mats to keep bowls in place on slippery floors and to help contain spills

- training treats or your pet's favorite everyday treats

- specialty foods, such as thistle or millet sprays for birds; fruit or vegetable pellets for small animals, like hamsters and gerbils; fish flakes or fish pellets; and live or frozen prey (like crickets) for reptiles

- veterinarian-approved bones or rawhide chews

- measured food scoop and airtight food storage bin to keep food fresh and pest-free

TOSS

These treats and feeding supplies:

- dishes that slide or are easily tipped over

- dishes that are too high or low for your pet to eat or drink from easily

- special water dishes that require batteries to keep a constant flow of water

- dishes and water bottles that are difficult to set up or fall out of holders

- dishes that cannot be cleaned properly

- water bottles and dispensers that leak

- treats or pet food your pet doesn't like or won't eat

- expired or recalled pet food and treats

- fish flakes that have gotten wet and might be contaminated

- frozen fish food that has thawed and is no longer safe to eat

---

Did you know?

It's a good idea to keep the phone numbers for your veterinarian, the closest 24-hour pet hospital, the Animal Poison Control Center number (888-426-4435), and the local pet rescue (in case your pet goes missing) in your phone's contact list. Also, keep a current photo of your pet so you can show it to searchers.

KEEP

These tanks, cages, crates, carriers, and accessories:

- indoor crate for when your pet needs solitude

- window perches for your cat to bask in the sun

- training or pet crates for containing your pet when you are not at home

- travel carrier that safely contains your pet for outings, trips to the veterinarian, vacations, or in the event of evacuation

- tank for fish, reptiles, or small critters that is a good size and offers room for your pet to grow

- cage that works well, like a bird cage with sliding doors that open to feed your bird

- paper cage liners that properly fit the size cage you own

- corn cob, woodchips, hay, or other bedding to line a cage for small animals

- rocks or gravel to fill the bottom of a fish or reptile tank

- nesting boxes for birds or small animals, like hamsters

- lighting for a tank, like hoods for fish tanks with the proper wattage and style lightbulbs, like incandescent versus fluorescent

- heating rocks or heating lamps, if needed for your pet

- filters and compatible filter inserts for your fish tank

- bubblers that add oxygen to the water

- submersible heater for your tropical or saltwater fish tank

- decorative backgrounds for your tank that adhere to the outside of the tank

- fish tank decor, like bubbling treasure chests, plastic rock formations, or coral pieces

- tank stands that fit tank sizes you own and use

- live plants that do well in the environment

- plastic plants that fish or animals like to hide around

TOSS
These tanks, cages, crates, carriers, and accessories:

- carriers, cages, crates, and tanks that are broken, missing pieces, or are no longer used

- tanks that leak because the silicone seals have deteriorated

- cardboard carriers that are not meant to be reused

- more carriers than the number of pets you own

- tanks that are missing the lid needed to prevent pets from escaping

KEEP

These collars and leashes:

- 1 collar that fits your pet properly and is the right length, weight, and width

- 1 durable leash with a working clasp (if you take your pet outside)

- 1 spare set in case something happens to the original

- ID tags with current information

- up-to-date licenses, as required by your town or state

TOSS

These collars and leashes:

- retractable leash that does not work properly

- retractable leash that has a thin cord instead of a wider belt, which can burn or injure your finger if it extends or retracts too quickly while touching you

- leash that allows the dog to roam farther from you than the law in your town allows

- leash that is rated too small to control your pet, based on weight

- leash that is uncomfortable for you to hold during a long walk

- fraying or damaged leashes that could snap or break

- collars or leashes that were part of a larger set and you don't use

- collars that can get caught on outdoor fences and trap your pet

- seasonal styles

KEEP

These toys, chews, and beds:

- bed, pillows, or sleeping pads that your pet actually uses

- heated pads for comforting puppies

- ergonomic foam pads for pets with sore joints

- chew toys that are in good condition

- toys your pet likes to play with

- toys that double as toothbrushes to help clean teeth and gums

- interactive fetch toys

- cat balls, mice, and other toys your cat finds entertaining

- wooden toys for small critters to gnaw on

- bird posts with sandpaper to keep nails trimmed

- mirrors that attract your bird

- balls of all sorts

- swings or slings for your pet to lounge

- play stands for activity time outside the cage

- tunnels that stay open and do not collapse on your pet

TOSS

These toys, chews, and beds:

- old or broken toys, which are unsafe for your pet, and those that are so chewed they have become potential choking hazards

- toys too worn to play with any longer

- squeaking toys or other noisy toys that are annoying

- catnip toys if you prefer your cat not have them

- toys meant to have food or treats added for extra playing time but now has residue that is impossible to clean

- plastic enclosed mazes or tube habitats that no longer fit together well or do not entertain your pet

- cuttlebone holder that does not fit the birdcage

KEEP THIS, TOSS THAT

- damaged birdcage covers

- battery-operated toys that need a replacement battery that is either too expensive or too difficult to find

- toys that don't deliver on their promise, like a toy that is supposed to dispense treats but does not work

- any toy or bed that has been recalled

KEEP

These grooming and cleaning supplies:

- shampoo and conditioner that works for your pet

- brush and/or comb that is easy to clean

- hair bows or neck bandannas if your pet tolerates them

- dental products for teeth and gums

- nail clippers that are easy to use and clip cleanly

- scissors or fur trimmers that are sharp and in good working order

- paw wipes to clean their paws without having to bathe them

- birdbath that is clean and sanitary

- spray bottles for birds and hermit crabs that deliver a fine mist

- cleaning pads and scrubbers that get the job done

- rubber gloves to keep your hands clean during cleanup jobs

- pet stain lifters and carpet cleaners

TOSS

These grooming and cleaning supplies:

- expired specialty shampoos

- scissors that are not sharp

- nail clippers that are difficult to use or leave a ragged edge

- sprayer hose faucet attachment for bathing your pet that does not attach properly or is missing parts

- styptic powder or pencils that have been improperly stored (if they have been exposed to moisture, sunlight, or temperatures greater than 82°F for three days or more, they may no longer be effective)

- rotating nail trimmer that frightens your pet

- tear stain wipes that are dried out and no longer useful

- algae drops for your fish tank that do not work as promised

- algae- and glass-cleaning magnets that are too much trouble to use

KEEP
These medications and supplements:

- first-aid supplies, like Benadryl, for allergic reactions

- flea and tick treatments

- tear stain supplements, if it applies to your pet

- vitamins (liquid or pill form)

- supplements your pet is taking, like hip and joint pills

- water-testing equipment

- water treatments, like dechlorinators

TOSS
These medications and supplements:

- cone collar from a previous medical condition

- leftovers from old procedures or surgeries, like unused gauze pads or bandages

- medication syringes or droppers for dispensing medication your pet no longer needs

- expired medications

- medications for pets you no longer own or for ailments your pet no longer suffers from

KEEP
These cleaning and other supplies:

- cleaning sprays

- deterrent sprays, like bitter-tasting solutions to prevent chewing

- litter box that is large enough for your pet

- kitty litter that is dust-free and easily scooped

- a good litter scoop

- cage lining or bedding, like wood chips

- pet waste pickup bags and bag dispenser that attaches to the leash

- pet waste scooper

- indoor potty-training pads, if needed

TOSS
These cleaning and other supplies:

- cracked litter scoops

- litter that is too dusty to use

- flushable litter that is not safe for you to flush down your plumbing

- litter boxes your pet will not use

- pet waste bags that are too thin to be useful

- potty-training pads that leak through or do not dry quickly

- fish-tank filters that no longer work

- cracked or damaged fish-tank air pump airline tubing

KEEP/TOSS CLUE: Keep a carrier for your pet, even if your pet doesn't travel regularly with you; any pet may have an unexpected trip to the veterinarian or need to be moved in the event of an emergency.

Chapter 4
Family and Living Room

Is your family room an inviting place to relax and unwind, or is it filled with clutter that stresses you out?

Even in this digital age of e-readers, many of us are lovers and savers of books. If you have run out of room on your bookshelf and find yourself stacking books next to the bookcase, you need to toss some today.

Speaking of the digital age, these days it seems devices are out of date as soon as you purchase them. Have you upgraded but forgotten to toss the original it replaced? What about remotes and accessories? All-in-one chargers or chargers that are compatible with multiple devices should be kept. An obvious toss is anything that belongs to something you no longer own.

Then there is the decor. Move each item out of its original position to allow your eye to see the space as clear and clutter-free. Then put back only the items you love to look at or the items you regularly use.

It all comes down to a few tosses to achieve an inviting family room—a room you can welcome company into without embarrassment or having to rush to clean up first.

Ask yourself these key questions:

1. Is it worth my time and energy to dust and clean around it?
2. Does this still interest me?
3. Is it a novelty item or impulse buy that was used once?

Let's get started now, and in just a little while, you can put your feet up and breathe a sigh of relief.

Entertainment

KEEP

These catalogs, magazines, and newspapers:

- only the current editions of the catalogs you most often order from or flip through

- today's weekday newspaper

- the latest weekend edition of the newspaper

- back issues (up to 12 months) of any magazine you find yourself referencing frequently, as this covers all seasons

TOSS

These catalogs, magazines, and newspapers:

- weekday papers that are more than a day old

- weekend papers that are more than a week old

- every catalog except the most recent issue

KEEP/TOSS CLUE: Did you know you can transfer a subscription to a friend, relative, hair salon, or doctor's office, even if it was gifted to you, by calling the subscription office and having the address changed? Magazines, new or dated, are also often welcomed by Laundromats. Ones that are appropriate for children might be accepted by day care centers and scouting troops for craft projects. And dated magazines can be given to the Alzheimer's units at nursing homes to be enjoyed by patients whose memories may be jogged by the photos.

KEEP
Books that:

- you reach for over and over again, like this one!

- you will read within the next year

- are signed by your all-time favorite author

- you use as reference for work or on game night, like a Scrabble dictionary

---

Did you know?

You can check the potential value of a book, like a collector's or first edition, at no charge by logging onto Biblio.com/book-value.

STORAGE SOLUTION
....
Bookcases look most balanced when they are filled 75 percent with books and 20 percent with decorative items, leaving 5 percent of empty space.

TOSS
Books that:

- you didn't enjoy reading the first time

- you will never read (these are the ones you pass over every time you reach for another)

- are duplicates (yes, we've all bought a book we already own)

- you have both the soft- and hardcover versions of (pick one to keep)

- seemed interesting at one time but you're not passionate about reading now

- don't belong to you (if you are still in touch with the original owner, return the book)

- are references you can more easily find online, like a dictionary and thesaurus

- are outdated like old encyclopedia sets or the original edition of *Keep This, Toss That*

- are advice books that you didn't find helpful or on topics from your past that you no longer need advice on (like parenting books if your children are grown)

- are textbooks, atlases, or maps that are more than a year old

- are damaged, musty, moldy, or have a binding too broken to be readable

---

Did you know?

From a design perspective, on an average coffee table (48" in length), it is suggested you keep three to five coffee table books on subjects you are interested in or books with covers that bring desired colors into your decor.

KEEP
Games and puzzles that:

- have all their pieces

- you and your family enjoy playing

TOSS
Games and puzzles that:

- have pieces missing

- are damaged or broken in any way (i.e., cards that are bent or ripped; electronic games that don't function)

- you never play

- have never been taken out of their shrink wrap

- are dangerous to play indoors, like darts

- are too difficult or take too long to play

- are too large to play or assemble in the space you have

KEEP

These media and entertainment items:

- the devices you reach for all the time, like your smartphone, which probably doubles as a camera, music player, and video camera

- remotes and chargers that are compatible with multiple devices

TOSS

These media and entertainment items:

- VHS tapes if you no longer own the player

- DVDs you never watched or that you will not watch again

- old cameras and video cameras

- phased-out cellphones

- orphaned stereo system components

- tape decks

- old or outdated cable boxes

- stereo or surround-sound speakers if your television has that capability built in

- video game discs that skip

- video game consoles, controllers, and discs that you no longer use

- remotes and chargers for devices you no longer own

Did you know?

There are services that will convert your slides, film reels, and VHS tapes to current technology for you. Check out the options at CostcoDVD.com, DVDWalmart.com, and Legacybox.com.

Decor

KEEP
Furniture that:

- you love

- fits in the room without making it feel cluttered

- offers great storage

- does double duty, like a storage ottoman that can also be used for additional seating

- is comfortable and fits your style

TOSS
Furniture that:

- is falling apart or broken beyond repair

- doesn't fit in the room

- is stained, torn, or uncomfortable

- you and your family have outgrown (like a child-size rocking chair)

- no longer serves a purpose (such as a CD tower if you've converted all your music to digital files and tossed the CDs)

---

12 Clever Ways to Use an Armoire

1. Craft and project area
2. Sewing cabinet
3. Linen closet
4. Storage for your entryway
5. Gardening and potting shed
6. Kid zone
7. Laundry "room"
8. Home office
9. Pantry storage
10. Shoe storage
11. Home bar
12. Bathroom vanity

KEEP

Candles and candleholders that:

- coordinate with your decor

- you can easily buy replacement candles for

- have a wick tall enough to light and continue burning

- fit holders you own (candles)

TOSS

Candles and candleholders that:

- are chipped, cracked, or have been glued together one too many times

- are "too pretty" to use or, conversely, not pretty enough to use

- always end up caked in melted wax, which takes a long time to remove

- are melted and out of shape

- are prone to tipping over and are therefore a fire hazard

KEEP

Three lamps or lights that:

- fit the space and work with your decor

- together offer the three points of light recommended by interior designers (floor lamp, tabletop lamp, and down lighting from the ceiling)

TOSS

Lamps or lights that:

- do not offer enough lighting to be useful

- are harsh and irritating to the eye, like lamps with bare bulbs

- you just do not like

- are fire hazards, like lamps that need rewiring

KEEP

These accessories and decor:

- artwork you love that is framed and fits on tabletops or works on walls

- artwork that still suits your style and decor

- throw pillows and blankets that are in good condition and used often

TOSS

These accessories and decor:

- artwork, figurines, and knickknacks that you no longer love to look at or clean around

- artwork that needs framing but you have no plans to frame and hang

- extra throw pillows and blankets that are threadbare, worn, stained, or otherwise damaged

---

Did you know?

You don't have to display all your artwork all the time. Rotating artwork is a great way to freshen up a space.

Did you know?

From a home-design perspective, the ideal throw-pillow scenario is three pillows on a loveseat or five pillows on a couch, with no one pillow being larger than 18".

KEEP

Plants and flowers that you:

- have room for

- can easily take care of

- still enjoy

- see thriving in the environment you have

TOSS

Plants and flowers that are:

- diseased or otherwise not faring well

- difficult to maintain

- overgrown or have outgrown the space

- dust and allergen collectors, such as faux greenery and dried flower arrangements

- toxic to pets if eaten (if you have pets)

Did you know?

Indoor plants are for more than just decoration—they can actually improve your indoor air quality. The most common species known for their air-cleaning abilities are the peace lily, philodendron, and spider plant.

KEEP

These three types of vases:

- a tall, wide cylinder that's ideal for displaying a large bunch of long-stemmed flowers, such as tulips or sunflowers

- a square vase for uniform bouquets of carnations or roses

- a cylindrical bud vase with a 1" opening, perfect for holding a single stem, such as a rose, calla lily, or orchid

KEEP/TOSS CLUE: A clever way to toss unnecessary flower vases is to fill them with flowers from your garden and give them away to friends and neighbors.

TOSS

Flower vases that:

- are cracked or chipped

- are not dishwasher safe and can't easily be cleaned by hand

- are stained beyond being able to be cleaned

- don't match your style or decor

- are not appealing to you

- are not a standard size, so flowers never look well arranged

- are made of thin glass that can easily crack

- don't have a weighty bottom or are too tall and therefore at risk of tipping over

- are round fishbowls (which are challenging for flower arranging)

- are difficult to add water to

Chapter 5
Kitchen and Dining Room

Having a kitchen that is organized and clutter-free starts with being realistic. Sometimes you just have to ask yourself, "Am I ever going to make homemade madeleines?" If the answer is no, then it is time to toss the madeleine pan. The kitchen/dining area is the heart of your home, where you spend lots of time and where company tends to congregate. Let's streamline it. Keep what you use and let the rest go.

Imagine opening a kitchen cabinet without worrying about coffee mugs toppling out. Picture the day when you can find the lid that matches the food storage container. That can be your reality with a few tosses from some key categories. It's all about balance, keeping the best of the multiples you own, and holding onto the things you need for the way you cook and entertain today. Is that fancy chocolate curler you bought on a whim still in the package? Guess what? That's a classic "toss" clue!

And let's not forget about your dining-room table if you have one—and if you can find it underneath the sea of paperwork and piles of stuff. So many of our memories start with sitting around a table and sharing meals with loved ones.

Ask yourself these key questions:

1. Does keeping this item make more work for me?
2. Could something else I own do the same job?
3. Is this item something I think I should own but never actually use?

It's time to whip up the kitchen area of your dreams.

Appliances

KEEP
One coffeemaker that:

- is simple to program

- starts automatically at a pre-programmed time

- brews how much you need, like directly into ready-to-go travel mugs

- has an easy-to-fill water tank

- automatically shuts off

- keeps brewed coffee piping hot

- indicates how long the brewed coffee has been sitting

- comes with a permanent filter

- takes up a small footprint on a kitchen counter

TOSS
Extra coffeemakers that:

- do not consistently brew tasty cups of coffee

- are missing the carafe because it broke and you never replaced it

- have a chipped or cracked carafe that is in danger of breaking

- should have been tossed when you upgraded or bought/received a replacement

KEEP/TOSS CLUE: Toss the machines (along with the tools and foods) that prepare foods you love to eat but will never prepare at home, like sushi or sno-cones. If you are selling the item, you'll get more when you sell it with the instruction manual included. If you can't find it, print one out from the manufacturer's website. Don't forget any accessories, attachments, and cords.

One toaster that:

- browns evenly and consistently even with back-to-back batches

- toasts quickly

- offers multiple settings for toasting

TOSS

Extra toasters that:

- have slots that are too thin for bagels

- do not pop up high enough to allow you to retrieve slices easily

- have hard-to-clean crumb trays

- leave crumbs all over the countertop

KEEP

One blender or food processor that:

- still has all its pieces and accessories

- you actually use more than twice a year

- breaks down tough ingredients, like kale leaves or flaxseeds

- has a strong motor

- produces a smooth puree

- crushes ice

- includes multiple blades that shred, chop, grate, and grind

- is large enough that you can blend everything in one batch

- is easy to clean or dishwasher safe

- has a BPA-free cup

- comes with a spill-proof, vented lid for adding ingredients while in operation

TOSS

Extra blenders or food processors that:

- don't do the job they claim they do

- consistently overheat

- require you to continually hold down a button for it to work

- are too noisy

- are not durable or reliable

- are missing parts that are too costly to replace

- are trendy or older versions that you don't use

KEEP

One ice-cream maker that:

- churns well and makes enough servings to suit your consumption

- has a large spout to prevent spills while adding ingredients

- has a double-insulated bowl to freeze ingredients quickly and evenly

- doesn't require prefreezing or rock salt (which you may not always have on hand)

- has a removable bowl and paddle for easy cleaning

- is easy to assemble and simple to use (i.e., no hand cranks)

- has a built-in timer and automatically stops when batch is complete to prevent overchurning or burning out the motor

- has an opening in the lid, allowing you to add mix-ins, like fruit, nuts, chips, and candy

- is relatively quiet (all make noise, but some are louder than others)

TOSS

Other appliances most ice-cream makers can replace:

- gelato maker

- sorbet maker

- slushie and other frozen drink makers

- frosty shake maker

- frozen yogurt maker

- frozen hot-chocolate maker

- frappe maker

KEEP/TOSS CLUE: At first it may seem counterintuitive to keep an ice-cream maker or waffle iron if you rarely, if ever, find yourself making homemade ice cream or a fresh waffle. But if that appliance can replace multiple others that serve a purpose you actually need, then you can keep it without ever using it for its originally intended purpose.

KEEP

One waffle iron that:

- has a locking latch for uniform thickness

- has a temperature-recovery function so it can make back-to-back waffles without waiting

- has built-in cord storage

- stores upright in little space

- has a waffle-ready indicator

- has an easy-to-clean overflow channel

- doesn't drip batter

- is easy to clean

- has a nonstick coating that is not flaking or scratched

TOSS

Other makers your waffle iron can replace:

- grilled cheese maker

- quesadilla maker

- calzone cooker

- bacon maker

- brownie pan

Did you know?

Your waffle iron can also cook French toast, hash browns, scrambled eggs, corn bread, cut-and-slice biscuits, falafel, cinnamon rolls, brownies, Monte Cristos, and cookies. Experiment with cooking times and temperatures, or log onto Pinterest and search "waffle maker uses" or Google "waffle maker _____" (insert the food you want to cook) to see how others have done it successfully. Or check out the book *Will It Waffle?* by Daniel Shumski.

KEEP

One slow cooker or multicooker that:

- has adjustable temperature control

- has a locking lid for travel

- is made of an easy-to-clean material, like ceramic

- has a removable insert for easy cleaning or even cleaning in the dishwasher

- has an insert that goes from stovetop or grill to slow cooker and dishwasher for true one-pot cooking

- is 5 quarts or larger, which is the perfect size for making multiple servings to cook and freeze meals, take to a party, or serve on a buffet line

TOSS

Other appliances your slow cooker or multicooker can replace:

- fondue maker

- buffet food warmer

- rice cooker

- vegetable steamer

- fish steamer

- risotto maker

- chili cooker

- fruit poacher

Pots and Pans

KEEP

These three essential pots and pans:

- 10-quart stockpot with lid to boil water for pasta or steaming vegetables and also for large batches of soups and stews. Keep the lighter version with easy-to-grasp handles, since you need to be able to easily and safely lift it when it is full of boiling water.

- 3-quart sauté pan with lid for searing meats, cooking chicken, risotto, and smaller batches of deep frying as well as stir-frying. Keep the one with higher sides to prevent spillovers.

- 2-quart saucepan with lid for reheating food, making sauce, cooking pasta, and boiling or steaming vegetables. Keep the one with a tight-fitting lid to help keep moisture in the food while cooking.

TOSS

Pots and pans that:

- have handles that are loose and cannot be tightened or that get too hot while cooking

- are missing the lid (if you only use the pot or pan with the lid)

- have nonstick coatings that are flaking or scratched

- heat unevenly, causing burn spots on the food

- are wobbly, warped, dented, or otherwise compromised

- are designed for a single purpose, such as "perfect" meatloaf pans, unless you use them often

- are oversized and do not fit well on your stove burners

- are too heavy

7 Basic Pans to Keep

1. **9" x 13" baking pan.** It is just as easy to bake a cake as it is to roast a chicken in this standard pan. Keep one with a lid, as it makes it easy to bake and take or store leftovers.

2. **9" x 9" square baking pan.** Perfect for brownies and bar desserts, this pan also fits in most toaster ovens when you need to cook or bake in the mini oven.

3. **10" round cake pan.** With two of these on hand, you can not only make a layer cake but also roast side-dish portions of vegetables—and much more.

4. **9" pie plate.** Not just for pies, this basic dish also works for quiche and refrigerated dinner rolls or cinnamon buns.

5. **9" x 5" loaf pan.** You can cook everything in this, from breads and cakes to stuffed meatloaf.

6. **Baking or jelly roll sheets.** These have lips, while cookie sheets do not, so cookies will not accidentally slide off. You can also use them to roast vegetables or bake fries and hors d'oeuvres.

7. **Muffin tin.** Essential for muffins and cupcakes, it can make perfectly portioned mini tarts, cheesecakes, meatloaves, mac and cheeses, or soufflés. Use the pan to freeze individual portions of soup or stock. Or flip it over to bake bread, tortilla, cheese, or bacon bowls or fillable cookie cups.

- have rivets or other parts that are difficult to clean properly

- are too small

- are the ones you bypass in order to grab your easy-to-use pots and pans

> ### STORAGE SOLUTION
> Use an extra muffin tin as a drawer organizer. Food containers missing lids also work for this purpose.

Cooking Utensils

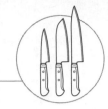

KEEP

These three knives:

- 10" serrated knife for slicing bread. This knife has a long, thin serrated blade that will slice through a loaf of bread without smashing it along the way. This knife steps in to slice super-ripe tomatoes, too, and does the job of a cake leveler.

- 8" chef's knife for large jobs. It also works well for smashing garlic, bruising herbs, and checking the "doneness" of baked goods.

- 3" paring knife for smaller jobs. This tiny paring knife takes on the jobs that other knives can't do, like peeling and segmenting citrus fruit into sections.

TOSS

These knives:

- specialty knives and single-purpose slicers

- dull knives that can't or won't be sharpened

- knives that are rusted, bent, chipped, or have tarnished blades

---

Did you know?

The 8" chef's knife is arguably the most versatile knife in the kitchen.

KEEP

One pair of kitchen shears with:

- soft, nonslip handles for a comfortable grip

- separating blades to allow for easy cleanup and to prevent food from collecting in crevices

- one blade that has minuscule serration, which prevents food from slipping

- an adjustable rivet that allows you to adjust the tension according to the job, so you can use the shears for everything from deboning chicken to slicing parchment paper

TOSS

Excess pairs of kitchen shears with:

- a wide tip that make small jobs difficult

- thin blades that bend and are less durable

- dull shears that don't get the job done and can't be sharpened

Did you know?

Save yourself added cleanup by using shears to cut foods, like parsley, directly into a pot or bowl.
Also, use a large bowl to collect the trash as you prep ingredients. Then dump the bowl one time instead of making multiple trips and dripping on the way to the garbage can.

Other tools your shears can replace:

- pita bread slicer (cut up to three stacked pitas simultaneously using shears)

- herb mincer (simply trim and chop herbs with shears)

- pie edger (once you drape the pie crust over the plate, use shears to trim)

- green bean snipper (use shears to snip the stems)

7 Essential Cooking Utensils

1. Spoonula

 Designed like a spatula with a deep well in the center and a highly flexible head, this can be used as a mixing spoon, a serving spoon, or a spatula. The best one is dishwasher safe and has a heat-resistant silicone head that bends enough to scrape and a sturdy handle with a comfortable grip.

2. Slotted spoon

Choose a spoon with many small slots that allow liquid to drain while preventing food from falling through.

3. Nonslotted spoon

Look for a nonslotted silicone spoon about 12" in length with a tapered point that allows you to scoop directly out of a 14-ounce can.

4. Whisk

A silicone or silicone-wrapped whisk allows you to whisk directly in a nonstick pan without causing damage. The 9" whisk is a universal size.

5. Ladle

A ladle that is 12" to 14" long ensures that you can reach the bottom of a tall stock pot without burning yourself. Make sure it has a sturdy neck that won't bend under the weight of the food.

6. Spatula (aka flipper/turner)

The spatula is perfect for flipping pancakes, among other foods. It features a wide, flat surface (around 11" x 3") that tapers to a thin edge to easily slide under delicate foods, like fish fillets or fried eggs. Heat-resistant silicone or nylon covering a stainless-steel core gives the spatula stability without risking damage to your nonstick pans.

7. Offset spatula

 An offset spatula, in which the blade is bent and sits about half an inch below the handle, is a must-have for icing cakes and cupcakes. It's also a lifesaver when it comes to serving pie or quiche slices with the crust intact. Choose one made of thin material, with a 10" to 12" blade.

KEEP

One 10" microplane grater that:

- has an ergonomic handle that allows it to hang (so you can keep a utensil with sharp edges out of the drawer)

- is made of stainless steel for easy cleanup

TOSS

The following graters:

- extra microplane graters in other sizes

- box graters

- cheese graters (if you always buy pre-grated cheese)

- spice graters

- citrus zesters

---

7 Foods You Can Grate with a Microplane Grater

1. Fresh coconut

2. Horseradish

3. Fresh ginger

4. Dried mushrooms

5. Dried hot peppers

6. Vegetables, like carrots, potatoes, zucchini, cucumber, cabbage, radishes, broccoli, onions, and cauliflower stems (for breads, pancakes, sauces, and slaws)

7. Butter (to quickly soften a frozen stick for a recipe)

KEEP

These two peelers:

- Y-shape, perfect for larger peeling jobs, like squash

- swivel blade, just right for smaller tasks like peeling apples

But only if they also:

- have a comfortable handle

- clean up well or are dishwasher safe

- have a sharp eyer for removing blemishes in one cut

TOSS

Peelers that:

- have a dull blade

- are difficult to clean properly

- offer an adjustable thickness option that does not work

KEEP/TOSS CLUE: If you want to hang on to a sentimental gadget (like a vegetable peeler used by your grandmother) that no longer works very well, blend it in with your kitchen decor as a piece of art. For example, you could place it in a clear mason jar on a kitchen shelf.

Did you know?

You can use your peeler to make fancy curls of chocolate to decorate desserts. You can also peel thin-skinned fruits, like mangoes, which wastes less fruit, and make ribbon "noodles" from fresh squash and zucchini.

KEEP

Two pairs of kitchen tongs with:

- silicone tips to ensure scratch-proof cooking

- rubber or silicone handles that stay cool to the touch and ensure your grip won't slip

- ridges along the tong edge to provide a secure grip on all foods

- dishwasher-safe material to save cleanup time

TOSS

Excess pairs of kitchen tongs with:

- metal tips, which can scratch pans

- metal handles, which conduct heat and therefore can burn unprotected hands and fingers

- crevices and grooves, which can become unsanitary because they're difficult to clean

- flimsy material, which are useless and actually dangerous

KEEP/TOSS CLUE: It is difficult to cook quickly and safely if you have to take time to sanitize while you are grilling, frying, or searing meat to prevent cross-contamination. A second pair of tongs comes in handy and saves you cleanup time.

STORAGE SOLUTION
....

No locking clasp on the tong handles? No problem. Simply slide the tongs into the cardboard tube from your empty roll of paper towels to prevent them from popping open inside a drawer.

Let's Play the Gadget Game

In this game, the fewer points you score, the better you do. Out of a possible 40 points (or more, if you have multiples), your goal is to get down to 10 or fewer points by reconsidering which gadgets you keep. Look over this list of popular gadgets, and give yourself one point for each one of these you own. (If you own multiples, each version counts as a point.)

Presses and peelers:

_____ asparagus peeler

_____ bacon press

_____ citrus press

_____ coffee press

_____ corn peeler

_____ crumb crust press

_____ garlic peeler

_____ garlic press

_____ grill press

_____ hamburger press

_____ kiwi peeler

_____ orange peeler

_____ plantain press

_____ shrimp peeler

_____ sushi press

_____ taco press

Zesters, reamers, and graters:

_____ chocolate grater

_____ citrus zester

_____ electric reamer

_____ citrus reamer

_____ nutmeg grater

_____ orange reamer

_____ orange zester

Corers, curlers, pitters, seeders, and hullers:

- _____ apple corer
- _____ avocado pitter
- _____ butter curler
- _____ carrot curler
- _____ cheese curler
- _____ cherry pitter
- _____ chocolate curlers
- _____ cucumber curler
- _____ cupcake corer
- _____ jalapeño seeder
- _____ olive pitter
- _____ pepper corer
- _____ pineapple corer
- _____ potato curler
- _____ strawberry huller
- _____ zucchini curler

_____ **Total**

KEEP/TOSS CLUE: Toss gadgets used to make the homemade version of something you typically buy ready-made. No judgment here! For instance, if you buy jars of chopped garlic because you prefer not to have to chop it, then you don't need that garlic press, after all.

KEEP/TOSS CLUE: Avoid purchasing sets! They are far from the bargain they appear to be. All you end up with is a subpar version of the one tool you wanted and about eleven more you didn't need and wouldn't have purchased if it were not for the set. Sets also tend to bring other unnecessary clutter like a block or container or drawer tray. Since it is "still good," you feel guilty tossing it, but then again, you never needed it in the first place! Avoid having to toss it later by not letting it into your house in the first place.

KEEP

One pizza wheel with:

- a 4" wheel, which is the most versatile size, and made of plastic, for use on every cutting surface, including a pizza stone

- a soft handle and thumb guard for a safe, comfortable grip

- a slick surface that will glide through crusts without dislodging toppings

- easy-to-clean pieces, which either come apart or are designed to prevent clogs, while leaving more of the blade exposed for thorough cleaning

TOSS

Excess pizza wheels that:

- are not sharp enough to cut without force

- are ergonomic or have arched handles meant to provide leverage (oftentimes making the wheel unwieldy to work with and therefore dangerous)

- have a loose center rivet that can't be tightened (or any other center pull that inadequately holds the wheel together or causes it to jar while rolling)

- scratch surfaces

---

14 Foods a Pizza Wheel Can Slice and Dice

1. Waffles and pancakes
2. Sandwiches
3. Chopped salads
4. Lattice pie crust
5. Doughs for bread, pizza, cookies, and more
6. Puff pastry
7. Fresh sheets of pasta
8. Lasagna
9. Quiche
10. Cooked spaghetti or long pasta (to make it kid-friendly)
11. Quesadillas
12. Meat, like ham steaks, chicken breasts, and hot dogs
13. Desserts, like brownies, sheet cakes, bar cookies, and fudge
14. Cloves of garlic, herbs, and green onions

KEEP

Two sets of good measuring spoons that:

- have measurements imprinted directly onto the spoon, so they don't wear off

- are stainless steel, so they won't tarnish over time and will never peel or warp with heat

- clean up easily, are dishwasher safe, and won't trap stains and odors

- are oval or have an elongated design, which is more useful, since it fits into spice jars and other containers

- are all one piece, which are typically a stronger construction and will last longer

- have all standard measurements: ⅓ tsp, ¼ tsp, ½ tsp, 1 tsp, and 1 tbsp

TOSS

Excess sets of measuring spoons with:

- measurements that are no longer legible (making it difficult to determine the correct spoon)

- a sliding guide that needs to be cleaned between every measurement (inconvenient when baking and cooking)

- cracked, stained, peeling, rusted, dented, warped, or otherwise compromised materials

- welds, which are less sanitary because they have crevices where food gets trapped

- handles that bend when full

- unusual measurements (like smidgen, pinch, and dash—just use your fingertips)

Did you know?

The tablespoon can double as a scooper (think seeds in pumpkins, papayas, tomatoes, and jalapeños) as well as a jar scooper (think cherries and olives).

KEEP
One set of sturdy measuring cups for dry ingredients that:

- nest together, conserving space

- are stainless steel (which is heat resistant and lasts longer than plastic)

- have these four basic measurements: ¼ cup, ⅓ cup, ½ cup, and 1 cup

- have an offset handle to allow you to more accurately level off dry ingredients

TOSS
Excess sets of dry measuring cups with:

- measurements that are no longer legible (over time the print can wash off, making them less useful)

- hard-to-clean cups

- damaged, bent, plastic, peeled, melted, warped, and stained cups

- rarely used single measurements, like ⅔ cup (two scoops from a ⅓ cup works just as well)

KEEP
One 2-cup liquid measuring cup that:

- has easy-to-read markings

- is made of glass, which is microwave-safe, so you can boil water, melt butter, or use a stick blender in it

- has a handle that is cool to the touch when the cup is hot

- has a no-dribble pour spout

- has an angled surface, which allows you to read measurements from above

TOSS
Extra liquid measuring cups that:

- have measurements that are no longer legible

- do not list key measurements, like ⅓ cup or ⅔ cup

- are chipped, cracked, or stained or have stress fractures or smells that can't be cleaned

- have handles that are cracked or that get hot or slippery

KEEP

One reusable decorator icing/piping bag with coupler assembly that:

- is coated in polyester, which prevents grease from seeping through so it won't stain

- is made of flexible nylon, which makes it easy to maneuver, bend, and twist to push the food out

- is 12" or 16" (these sizes do not need to be refilled as often)

- comes with these three icing tips (to get almost every job done):

   Round tip. Best for filling and piping in areas; writing and printing messages; and for dots, beads, string work, and flower centers.

   Star tip. Best for stars, rosettes, and flowers. Using a tip numbered 15–20 allows you to make one-squeeze flowers, which are the easiest to do. The number of cuts on the end of the tip determines the number of petals the flower will have.

   Rose tip. Best for turning the decorator bag into a multipurpose tool. This tip has a large opening, making it easy to use with other types of fillings.

Did you know?

You can use a decorator bag without the tip for larger results. Without the tip in place, more food flows out for larger items, like cream puffs, éclairs, macaroons, meringue cookies, pasta shells (cannelloni and manicotti), and even cannoli shells.

TOSS

Extra decorator icing/piping bags that:

- are disposable

- have weak bag seams (which have the potential for messy explosions and blowouts that can ruin a project)

KEEP

One 1-tbsp spring-action scoop that:

- releases food easily

- is made of dishwasher-safe, noncorrosive stainless steel

TOSS

Extra scoops that:

- are difficult to squeeze or have a band that doesn't glide easily

- have a handle that is not easy or comfortable to hold

---

18 Clever Uses for a Spring-Action Scoop

1. Assembling sandwiches, like tuna or chicken salad

2. Filling foods, like homemade ravioli, stuffed peppers, and crescent pastries

3. Forming uniform-sized cookies for consistency and even cooking

4. Stuffing peppers, cabbage, and grape leaves

5. Scooping risotto for fried risotto balls

6. Making chocolate truffles

7. Forming brownie and cake pops

8. Forming dessert balls, like Rice Krispie treats or popcorn balls

9. Making meatballs and falafel balls

10. Making hushpuppies (use the scoop to drop batter quickly into oil to cook at the same time)

11. Portioning pancake batter

12. Making sliders

13. Making ice-cream sandwiches with waffles or cookies as the sandwich part

14. Forming uniform-sized biscuits

15. Forming crab cakes

16. Forming dumplings

17. Seeding fruits and vegetables

18. Filling your decorator's bag with thicker types of fillings, like purees and mousses

Dishes and Serving Ware

KEEP

Pieces for every day and formal place settings that:

- you love and that match your style and decor

- are chip-resistant

- are dishwasher- and microwave-friendly

- are flatware that is easy to grasp

- don't have hard-to-clean embellishments on the handles

TOSS

Pieces for every day and formal place settings that:

- are heavy and difficult to carry, especially when full

- you never use because they can't go in the dishwasher or are too difficult to clean (such as dishes with intricate embossing onto which food sticks)

- are too heavy or too light to enjoy eating with

- are stained, scratched, cracked, or chipped

- give food an unpleasant taste when you eat with them

- are spoons or forks that are too large to eat with

KEEP/TOSS CLUE: Keep one place setting of your choice, formal or informal, for each seat you have at the dining table when you have the table leaf inserted into the table. Also keep enough for guests that may be seated at folding tables.

To determine the total number of mugs and glasses to keep, multiply the number of people in the house who use glasses and mugs by how many days between washing dishes.

KEEP

Everyday cups and glasses that are:

- the most versatile size, 16 ounces, which provide enough room to add ice, if desired

- stackable when stored away

- dishwasher safe or easy to clean by hand

- ergonomic and easy to hold

- comfortable to drink from

TOSS

Everyday cups and glasses that are:

- broken, chipped, or otherwise compromised

- etched, ribbed, or octagon-shaped, making them hard to clean

- decorated with a printed design or colored film that is flaking, rubbing, or washing off

---

What You Need to Set the Table

For an informal place setting:

- 12" dinner plate
- Dinner fork
- Dinner knife
- Soup spoon
- Salad fork
- Cup
- Saucer

If you serve buffet style:

- 6½" dessert plates for appetizers, desserts, or cocktails
- Utensils as needed

For a formal place setting, add:

- Bread plate
- Salad plate
- Soup/pasta bowl
- Dessert plate
- Charger
- Butter knife
- Fish fork
- Fish knife
- Dessert fork
- Teaspoon

KEEP THIS, TOSS THAT

- stained, foggy, or scratched

- mismatched

- too delicate for comfortable use

- depressed at the base, so water pools, making them difficult to dry

- narrow at the base and prone to tipping

- souvenirs, such as the shot glasses that came home with you from your vacation or cheap plastic stadium cups

- gimmicky (like the hat with beverage can holder and bendy straw that reaches your mouth)

- smaller sizes, like 8 ounces or 12 ounces, since you can drink smaller amounts out of larger glasses

KEEP
Coffee mugs that:

- are the right size for the amount of drink you like to pour at once

- are in good repair without any chips or cracks

- have a secure handle

- regulate the temperature of the drink evenly (some mugs keep the drink hot way too long or allow the drink to cool too quickly)

TOSS
Coffee mugs that:

- are chipped, cracked, or stained

- you got as free promotions, souvenirs, or gifts

- you pass over in favor of your go-to favorites

- still have the price sticker on them or are still in the box

- are too thick or thin, too heavy or too light to be comfortable to drink from

---

Did you know?

Tossing #1 mugs of all kinds (teacher, nurse, Mom, Dad, etc.) does not make you less than number one. Keep only the ones that are truly meaningful to you.

KEEP

Wineglasses that:

- are thin-walled, which means you taste wine and not glass

- have a 20-ounce egg-shaped bowl, which works for both red and white wines, giving them room to breathe

- are colorless and unadorned

- are inexpensive and easily replaceable

- are not too heavy to be uncomfortable to hold while mingling with guests

- are short enough to fit in the storage space you have

TOSS

Wineglasses that:

- have a narrow base and are prone to tipping

- have such thick glass that you taste the glass more than the wine

- dribble when you drink, because they have a straight rim as opposed to a rim that is slightly curved inward

KEEP

One of each of these four types of serving platters:

- square 12" platter for desserts or main dishes

- oval 16" platter for serving a whole chicken, plus roasted vegetables

- large 12" serving bowl for mixed pasta or a really big salad

- large 16" cutting board that can double as a cheese board and appetizer platter

TOSS

Serving platters that are:

- cracked, chipped, stained, or otherwise compromised

- disposable

- too large to fit in your refrigerator, to be easily stored, or to be carried when they're loaded with food

- odd colors, styles, sizes, or that otherwise do not fit with your entertaining style or decor

KEEP

Travel mugs that:

- are insulated to retain the hot or cold temperature of your drink

- have a tight-fitting lid that is easy to put on, along with a gasket that prevents leaks and spills

- are constructed of stainless steel, making them durable and preventing them from retaining smells and tastes

- are double-wall insulated to prevent cold drinks from sweating

- have a shaker ball inside if you use the mug to mix powdery drinks

- you can easily drink from without dribbling

- fit in your car cup holder

- are large enough for the amount of drink you like (most are 12 ounces, but the more popular option is 16 ounces)

TOSS

Travel mugs that:

- are ceramic or glass, which can break easily

- have a hard-to-clean opening

- are too hot to handle when filled with a hot liquid

- don't fit in your car or other cup holder

- are unstable and tip easily

- are uncomfortable to carry

- are hard to clean or hand-wash only

- are not microwavable

- have features you don't use, like the travel mug that plugs into the cigarette lighter of your car to keep your beverage warm

- have a smell that won't go away

KEEP
Water or portable drink bottles that:

- have an internal filter that filters your water directly in the bottle

- fit cubes of ice in the mouth opening

- include a flavor infuser for infusing fruits or herbs into your water

- allow you to prefreeze the bottle to keep it colder longer

- have a tight seal so they don't spill

- keep drinks cold like they should

- are easy to clean

- are dishwasher safe

- are BPA-free

- fit in the lunch tote you most commonly use

- are meant for specific purposes, like to fit on a bicycle

- are stainless steel (if you are concerned about using plastic versions)

TOSS
Water or portable drink bottles that:

- have a drink opening that is too large or too small to dispense liquid properly

- are dirty beyond cleaning

- don't fit in your car's cup holder

- tend to sweat and make a mess

- tip over when stored

- are multiples of the same bottle that you aren't using, like four free promotional bottles from a charity event

KEEP/TOSS CLUE: Keep two travel mugs and water bottles per family member who uses one at least once a week. Keep only one per family member if they are used less often.

KEEP

Food storage containers that:

- are stackable for space-saving storage

- are different sizes but have interchangeable lids

- are airtight to keep stored foods fresh for the longest possible time

- do not leak, even if a broth or stew is stored inside

- are easy to clean or dishwasher safe

- are BPA-free

- are square (which saves more space than round containers)

- are clear, so you can easily see what is stored inside

- have secure-fitting lids

- have removable gaskets for complete and easy cleaning

TOSS

Food storage containers that:

- don't seal tightly

- are repurposed margarine tubs, yogurt containers, salad bar or deli containers (which were not designed to stand up to repeated uses or meant to be microwaved)

- have burned, bubbled, or warped spots

- are cracked or scratched

- are stained with no hope of coming clean

- are odd and not useful sizes

- have a lingering food odor

- don't have lids, have lids that are difficult to remove, or have lids with broken-off tabs

How Many Containers Should You Keep?

These should cover all your leftovers:

- 12 identical, clear, 16-ounce containers (about 6"x 6"x 6") with matching lids. Clear containers allow you to easily see what you've stored, and when they're all the same size, they stack neatly in the refrigerator (with the lids on) and in the cupboard (with the lids off)

- 4 large or extra-large rectangular containers for big-batch meals, like lasagna, or for when you want to freeze a meal for later or bring someone a casserole

Keep these for lunch-packing needs:

- 3 square sandwich-size containers (that fit in your lunch tote) per family member who totes a meal at least once a week

- 3 square containers with interior compartments

- 2 mini condiment containers per family member who totes a salad or dish that needs a condiment

Choose glass if you:

- are concerned about the health or environmental impact of using plastic containers

- are using them mostly to store leftovers at home

- tend to store strong-smelling foods like garlic or potentially staining foods like marinara sauce

- prefer to reheat food in the microwave

Choose plastic if you:

- frequently tote food to work or potlucks

- tend to lose or give away your containers

- have young children helping in the kitchen and don't want to worry about breaking glass

KEEP THIS, TOSS THAT

Food

KEEP
Dried spices and herbs that:

- you reach for time and time again

- give off an aroma when crumbled between your fingers, indicating freshness

These are common go-to spices and herbs:

- spice blends you use frequently, like lemon pepper or Italian seasoning

- basil
- bay leaves
- cayenne
- cinnamon
- crushed red pepper
- onion powder
- oregano
- paprika

If you enjoy preparing more worldly cuisines, also keep these:

- coriander
- cumin
- curry powder
- fennel
- nutmeg
- rosemary
- sage
- tarragon
- thyme
- turmeric

TOSS
Bottles of dried spices and herbs:

- that have been open for six months (if ground) or one year (if whole)

- whose color has faded

- that have clumped or whose texture has changed

- are past their "best by" dates

KEEP

These top ten condiments that you probably reach for over and over:

- barbecue sauce
- hot sauce
- ketchup
- mayonnaise
- mustard
- ranch dressing
- relish
- soy sauce
- steak sauce
- Worcestershire sauce

TOSS

Condiments that:

- came with takeout or that you brought home from a restaurant—especially if you don't remember how long ago you brought them home
- are past their "sell by," "use by," or "best by" dates
- were opened but not stored according to the manufacturer's directions
- you tried but just don't like enough to continue using
- you have too little left of and no idea what to do with it
- are no longer in your diet plan

STORAGE SOLUTION

Keep red spices in the fridge to extend their life. Paprika, chili powder, and other spices in the red pepper family will remain fresher longer when stored in the refrigerator.

Cooking References

KEEP

Cookbooks and cooking magazines that:

- you currently reference regularly, such as a specific diet book

- have stains, smears, and crinkled pages—that means you're using them!

- contain recipes you actually prepare and can't easily find online

- rely on specific appliances you still own, like the tiny cookbook that came with your slow cooker

TOSS

Cookbooks and cooking magazines that:

- are more than a year old and not used

- have similar recipes to cookbooks or cooking magazines you use regularly

- have recipes that don't fit your lifestyle

- have recipes that are too complicated to prepare, require special equipment, have too many budget-busting one-use ingredients, or that you would rather buy than make

- don't have a single stain—a telltale sign they are not often used

STORAGE SOLUTION

Congratulations! In an effort to curb clutter, you clipped or photocopied recipes from cookbooks and magazines. Only now you're left with a bunch of loose recipes you never prepare. After tossing as many as you can by following the above checklist, stick the keepers in a three-ring binder organized roughly by category (soups, salads, and so on). Or snap photos and organize them using a recipe app like Pepperplate. com. If you want to get really fancy or have family recipes to pass along, you can upload the recipes to a service like CreateMyCookbook.com and, as it says, create your own cookbook.

Cooking and Dining Accessories

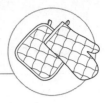

KEEP
Two sets of pot holders that:

- allow you to feel what you are holding

- have an excellent grip, like ones with silicone grips

- are washable

- are flame retardant

- are heatproof

- are flexible enough to conform to the task at hand

TOSS
Pot holders that:

- are more decorative than useful

- are as-seen-on TV potholders that do not deliver on their promise

- are grungy, ratty, or have holes in them

- are cumbersome, bulky, and difficult to get your hands into and out of

- do not have a grip, which means the item can slip out of your hand more easily

- can no longer be cleaned

- are oversized, so storing is a problem

- are fraying, with the edges coming undone or the interior separating

KEEP
Seven dish towels that:

- are absorbent

- leave a streak-free, lint-free surface

- are bleachable when necessary

- are machine washable

TOSS

Dish towels that:

- are too small to be efficient or useful

- don't launder well

- leave lint on things you launder them with

- are shrunken, bleach stained, or threadbare

- are too decorative to be practical

- don't absorb well

KEEP

Up to six trivets and hot plates that:

- can accommodate the size and weight of the dishes you place on top

- are easily cleaned

- are short enough to ensure they don't tip over when a hot dish is placed on them

- are in good repair, with no crumbling cork, rust, or damage

- are made of a heat-resistant material, like cork, bamboo, travertine stone, or silicone

- are still your color and style

- have rubber grips to prevent them from sliding when a hot dish is placed on them

- properly protect surfaces from heat

TOSS

Trivets and hot plates that:

- have scorch marks

- are wobbly or have missing feet

- scratch surfaces

- are more decorative than functional

- you don't use (more than six is excessive)

- are made of metal, which can conduct heat and scorch surfaces, or cause dishes to crack

KEEP

Place mats that:

- are washable

- catch crumbs instead of letting them fall through

- can be used outdoors if you dine al fresco

- don't melt under a hot plate

- are easy to store either flat or rolled

- are durable

- are proportionate in size to your dishes—too large a plate on too small a mat and crumbs fall off

- are not so expensive that you're nervous to use them

- are a color or pattern that can be dressed up for every season

TOSS

Place mats that:

- are slippery

- stain easily

- are peeling or have lifting edges

- don't match your decor

- are too small or too large for your table

- are not the right style for your table

- are seasonal specific (unless you really remember to put them out)

- are misshapen, shrunken, or warped

- come in a set that doesn't have enough for all the place settings you need

KEEP

These table linens:

- 2 casual and 2 formal tablecloths (and a table liner if the cloth is not water resistant)

- 2 sets of coordinating casual napkins and 2 sets of coordinating formal napkins. (You'll need 1 napkin per place setting, plus 2 for spares.) To calculate the number of place settings, count up the number of seats at your table when the leaf is in place (if you have one). Also include the number of seats at a folding table if you tend to set up for extra dinner guests.

As long as they:

- are easy to launder or inexpensive to have cleaned

- are in colors and styles that fit your current decor

- work with table sizes you currently own

- coordinate with other table linens you own, like napkins or a table runner

TOSS

Table linens that:

- were hung inside plastic dry-cleaning bags too long and now have an unpleasant chemical smell that washing will not remove

- are dingy, well worn, permanently discolored, or faded

- are too "nice" to use (you won't be able to enjoy your meal for fear something will spill on the cloth)

- slide off the table or require special padding underneath or unattractive overlays on top to protect the cloth and/or the table

- are in sizes for tables you no longer own

- are styles that you won't use

KEEP/TOSS CLUE: Basic napkin rings can be used year-round. Dress them up with holly sprigs in the wintertime or roses in the summer. There's no need for seasonal rings.

Chapter 6
Bedrooms and Clothing

Do you dream of a relaxing retreat, but the reality is your bedroom is a cluttered nightmare? Flat surfaces like nightstands and dressers quickly become junk hot spots. Worn-once clothing gets draped over every chair, and your closet is so jam-packed with clothes, you can never find anything to wear.

It probably won't surprise you to learn that the clothes closet is usually the biggest problem spot. Clothing can be an emotional issue. For instance, you may be holding on to clothes and shoes because they remind you of a special date, they were very expensive, or you think one day you'll be back in that size again. We've all kept clothes well past their prime, but there comes a time when you need to make choices. If you love to curl up in a threadbare sweatshirt that feels like a hug, then hold on to it. But if you are keeping it wishing it were in better condition, then let it go.

Today is the day to toss the clothes you don't love so you can enjoy the ones you do. Follow these keep/toss lists, customizing for your personal preferences, to transform your bedroom into a spacious haven.

Ask yourself these key questions:

1. If I saw it in a store today, would I buy it again at full price?
2. Does it make me feel great to wear it?
3. Is the item in good condition? Does it have stains or tears? Is it pilling, fading, fraying?

Create that calm space you crave, which will hopefully lead to a better night's sleep, in turn giving you more energy.

Bedroom Furniture and Accessories

KEEP

These pieces of furniture:

- your bed

- furniture that you use, like a dresser or armoire if you prefer to fold most of your clothes rather than hang them

- multifunction furniture that serves dual purposes, like a cushioned storage bench for seating and storage

- bedside table or wall shelf

- chest or trunk as a decorative storage option

- full-length mirror

- TV stand (if you have a television in your bedroom that is not wall-mounted)

TOSS

Pieces of furniture that:

- you do not use, like a vanity table if you put your makeup on in the bathroom

- have become clutter or dust collectors rather than functional, like a lounge chair that you throw your clothing on

- are falling apart

- have drawers that won't open or doors that are missing or off the hinges

- you no longer like or that you or other family members have outgrown

- serve a purpose you have no need for, like a TV stand if your television is mounted directly on the wall

- don't serve a purpose, like throw rugs

KEEP/TOSS CLUE: Just because pieces came together in a set does not mean you have to keep them together. For example, a dresser might work better in a dining room as a sideboard, or a nightstand may be more useful as a side table in the living room.

KEEP
These bed pillows:

- 1 or 2 sleeping pillows per bed that are less than 18 months old; after that, they should be replaced

- specialty pillows, like neck rolls or wedge bolsters for propping yourself up in bed

- 1 travel pillow per traveler, which can be stored in luggage

TOSS
Bed pillows that:

- are uncomfortable

- are past their prime (ideally, pillows should be replaced every 18 months)

- are lumpy or bumpy or the filling has clumped

- are too thin or flat

- do not circulate air well, making them too hot to sleep on

- irritate you or your allergies or have a chemical smell

- hurt your neck or head

- clutter the bed, like excessive quantities of accent pillows (three is a good stopping point)

- are stained, faded, or have ripping seams

- are too ornate to be properly washed without damaging the embellishments

- are handmade or cross-stitched but are tired, worn, or fraying

KEEP/TOSS CLUE: Based on your sleep style, keep the pillow that best supports your head in what is known as "neutral alignment," meaning your head is in line with your neck, or the pillow that has been specifically recommended for any medical conditions you have. Here are general guidelines:

- Back sleeper—medium support

- Side sleeper—firm or extra firm support

- Stomach sleeper—soft support

- Combination sleeper—medium support

KEEP THIS, TOSS THAT

KEEP

These decorative items:

- artwork that has sentimental value or brings you joy

- framed photographs of loved ones

- souvenirs that still bring you fond memories

> **KEEP/TOSS CLUE:** To keep the wall from feeling cluttered, stick to the common two-thirds formula: Frames or other items on the wall should fill two-thirds of the space over a piece of furniture. If you hang multiple frames, aim for 2" between each, and always try to group in odd numbers.

TOSS

These types of decor:

- photo frames that are no longer your style

- artwork that looks cluttered on the wall

- knickknacks that collect dust and are difficult or time-consuming to clean

- anything that has been glued back together one too many times

KEEP

The following types of light:

- lamps that provide proper lighting for your purpose, like a natural lamp for makeup application or one that is bright enough to read by

- a motion-activated nightlight that illuminates your path

- romantic or soothing lighting not fit to read by but perfect for relaxing

- a light inside the clothes closet so you can easily find shoes on the floor and tell black and navy blue pants apart

TOSS

Lamps that:

- are cluttering up dresser tops and bedside tables

- do not allow for lightbulbs that are bright enough to be useful

- are not your style or you just don't like

KEEP

Alarm clocks that:

- keep the correct time

- have a battery backup to ensure they go off even if the power has gone out

- automatically restore the time/date and alarm settings after power loss

- have optional dual alarms and weekend skip option

- offer the option of two separate settings if two people have to wake up at different times

- offer the option of waking up to something gentler than a beep tone, like light or progressive chimes, or plugging in your music player

- are loud enough to wake you up if you are a heavy sleeper

TOSS

Alarm clocks that:

- have such a bright display light that it interrupts your sleep

- startle you awake with a loud beeping

- are difficult to program

- have a display that is hard to read

Did you know?

It is not recommended to use your cell phone as an alarm clock. Having the phone so accessible makes it tempting to check it right before bed, which can wind you up when you should be winding down, or first thing in the morning, which jumps you into your day before you've even brushed your teeth. Your bedroom should be a place where you "disconnect."

Keeping Your Bedside Table Clutter-Free

 Your bedside table is not meant to be a catchall for stacks of unread magazines. Ideally, your bedside table should store only what you need for any romantic or relaxing in-bed activities. If other things pile up there, try storing them somewhere away from the bed. For instance, on top of your dresser, place a jar for loose change or a small box to collect receipts. On the table, you might keep:

- air purifier

- alarm clock

- humidifier/ dehumidifier

- jewelry dish

- lamp

- television remote control

- treasured framed photograph

- water bottle

And stored in drawers, a basket you slip underneath the table, or in decorative stacking boxes:

- craft project like a cross-stitch

- eyeglasses

- eye mask

- flashlight (in case of power outage)

- lip balm

- lotion

- nightly necessities (anything you use in your nightly routine)

- pen and notepad

- reading material/ books

- tissues

Clothing

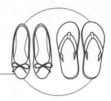

KEEP

Clothing that:

- you wear frequently

- is in good repair (not damaged, ripped, torn, missing buttons, or has a broken zipper)

- is comfortable to wear and doesn't itch, scratch, or pinch

- is flattering in style, cut, and color

- goes with at least three other things in your wardrobe

- can be worn to more than one place

- needs tailoring or can be resized, and you're willing to pay for it

- is easy to iron

- suits your lifestyle (if you work from home, you don't need six high-end designer suits)

- is formalwear and still fits, even if it only gets worn once or twice per year

TOSS

Clothing that:

- you have multiples of in one specific category, like five black turtlenecks

- you equate with bad memories

- is faded or has a smell that cannot be washed out

- was a gift but it is not "you"

- has been sitting in a pile for weeks (to-be-washed pile, to-be-ironed pile, to-be-hung-up pile)

- you consider "someday" clothes, as in "someday it will fit" or "someday I'll wear it"

- is annoying to wear (like if you're always pulling it up or tugging it down)

- you can't even remember buying

- irritates your skin or is uncomfortable

- you planned to return but never did and now it's too late

- still has tags on it and you have no plans to wear it in the next thirty days

- you will no longer wear for any reason

- you are embarrassed to wear in public

- you just feel tired of seeing yourself in

STORAGE SOLUTION

Keep special-occasion clothing, like costumes and holiday sweaters, stored with related items, such as holiday decorations, so you won't forget you have them.

KEEP/TOSS CLUE: Clothes you haven't touched in two years need to go. The two-year rule accounts for warmer-than-usual winters or unseasonable summers when you may not wear something you'd usually wear. It also accounts for clothes you've been saving for chores like yard work or painting, without letting you hold on to these items indefinitely.

KEEP/TOSS CLUE: If you're not willing to take the time to try something on to confirm that you still love it, then you can let it go.

KEEP
Active wear that:

- fits and still has enough support (like sports bras)

- allows you to work out comfortably

- is made from quick-dry moisture-wicking material

- is easy to hand wash or can go in the washing machine

TOSS
Active wear that:

- doesn't fit properly, is too constricting, or makes you feel self-conscious when wearing

- has seams that chafe or irritate your skin

- is the wrong weight or thickness for the season or type of workout

KEEP

Bras, underwear, shapeware, and lingerie that:

- are convertible and can be worn under a variety of outfits

- deliver on their promise

- don't have bothersome scratchy lace or itchy tags that cannot be removed

- are easy to care for or go in the washing machine

- wear smoothly under clothing without any lumps or bumps

- won't show under thin material or light colors

TOSS

Bras, underwear, shapeware, and lingerie that:

- you pass over time and time again

- you wouldn't want anyone to see you in

- are too large or too small

- are faded, ripped, stretched out, or the elastic is shot

- are uncomfortable for any reason

- show under clothing when you wear them (such as with panty lines)

KEEP

These nine dresses:

- Cocktail
- Sheath
- Daytime
- Sundress
- Formal
- Sweater
- Wrap
- Little black
- Maxi

Make sure the dresses you keep have:

- the correct hemline for the occasions to which you'll wear them (you don't want the sundress you'll wear to a baby shower to be mid-thigh)

- the proper material for their style (for example, you don't need sequins covering your daytime dress)

- the ability to be styled in multiple ways so they look different and work for many occasions

If you work outside the home, keep:

- A workplace-appropriate semicasual dress

- Something that works with a sweater or blazer in air-conditioned offices

- A dress that is comfortable while sitting at a desk all day

TOSS

Dresses that:

- require a slip or an uncomfortable undergarment if you prefer not to wear one

- are so low-cut they require a camisole underneath for modesty

- are so short you are self-conscious

- are from a specific occasion, like a bridesmaid dress that you will never wear again

---

STORAGE SOLUTION

Only keep clothes in your closet that currently fit you. If your weight fluctuates or you're honestly in the process of losing weight, keep one size up and one size down, but store it by size and category. Instead of lumping all the clothes in a single storage tote, group similar categories, like size 10 tops, size 10 bottoms, size 16 tops, and size 16 bottoms. That way, no one storage container gets too heavy, and when you are ready, you can easily pull what you need to keep or toss.

KEEP

Twelve neckties if you wear a tie every day (five if you only wear ties occasionally) that:

- are different enough in design or color to warrant keeping them

- are seasonal if you like to dress for the occasion (with a turkey tie on Thanksgiving, for instance)

- are classic colors that work with the majority of your shirts, like blue, green, red, or gold

- have timeless patterns, like striped, dotted, plaid, paisley, and tartan

- you get complimented on

- are well-constructed of a quality material

- are cravat (pretied) or clip-on if you are unable to tie a proper tie

TOSS

Extra ties that:

- are too similar to wear on back-to-back days without looking like you are wearing the same tie two days in a row

- don't match shirts or suits you own

- are prone to creasing

- are cheaply constructed or cheap looking

- are too trendy, too skinny, too wide, or hopelessly out of fashion

- are too bright, too cute, too funky, too casual, or just not your style

- have lost their shape or have rips, pulls, or stains

- are clip-ons that are obviously fake or have broken clips

KEEP/TOSS CLUE: For more formal occasions, keep a bow tie and three pocket squares that match ties you own.

KEEP

Business suits that:

- work for your current needs (if your office is casual or you wear a uniform to work, you don't need as many suits)

- have vented sides or back and a notched collar for easy movement

- are made of fabric that you feel comfortable in, e.g., it's not too shiny or itchy

- fit all over, including the shoulders

- are dark in color, making them more versatile

- are timeless in style

- resist creasing

- are easy to clean

TOSS

Business suits that:

- are made from a material you don't wear, like tweed

- have big bold buttons, patch elbows, too skinny or overly thick lapels, or other style accents that you don't like or are outdated

- have a memorable pattern (you can't wear it as often as a solid color or generic pattern)

KEEP/TOSS CLUE: Vests can be worn in lieu of a jacket or even with a button-down shirt and dressy jeans. If this style works for you, keep two vests.

STORAGE SOLUTION

Suits take up a lot of closet space. If you don't wear them on a regular basis, store them in another closet such as a guest room.

Did you know?

The average tuxedo rental is $150, so it makes sense to keep a full black tie ensemble. Even if you only wear it every three years, an average set pays for itself after only three wearings.

The F's and S's of Clothes to Keep

The clothes most easily reached in your closet should check all the boxes in the 3 F's and the 3 S's.

❑ **FIT** – Does it fit the way you dress today? Does it fit your job, volunteer, and leisure activities? Does it fit who you are and how you want to represent yourself to the world?

❑ **FLATTER** – Is it your color and cut? When you put it on, do you feel great wearing it? Do you get compliments when wearing it?

❑ **FUN** – Is it fun to wear and easy to care for? If it pinches, pulls, or is otherwise uncomfortable to wear, then you won't. If it is hand-wash, reshape, and lay flat to dry and you don't have time for that, then you won't wear it.

❑ **SEASON** – Is it wearable this current season? Out-of-season clothes need to be moved out of the way.

❑ **STYLE** – Is the item in style and is it your style? Is it a piece you really love or did you buy it just to try a trend?

❑ **SIZE** – Is it your current size or in the range of your current size? I know all too well that things can fluctuate, but be honest with yourself.

KEEP

Jackets and blazers that are:

- easy to move in

- versatile enough to coordinate with multiple other articles in your wardrobe

- easy to slip on and off without the lining becoming dislodged

TOSS

Jackets and blazers that are:

- too tight to be buttoned up

- hopelessly out of style

- too boxy or otherwise unflattering in style, cut, or color

KEEP

Pants that are:

- in colors that work with other items in your wardrobe

- flattering in style and look

- well-fitted—not too tight or too loose

- cut to fit the occasion, like a wide boot cut versus a skinny leg

- a length that works with the heel height you wear them with

TOSS

Pants that:

- are worn out but you are keeping until you can find a replacement

- have a zipper that does not function properly

- have a button fly that is difficult to work with

- are see-through and make you self-conscious

- none of your shoes will work with

- have pleats or pockets that add unnecessary bulk around your midsection

KEEP

These five types of jeans:

- trouser jeans, which work with a bunch of outfits

- jeans in true blue or a dark wash, which are more slimming colors

- white jeans, which can be casual or dressed up

- jeans to wear with flats

- jeans to wear with heels

As long as they also:

- have a midrise waist, which is the most universally flattering style

- have a flat front, to avoid extra bulk in the mid area

- are styled with larger pockets that are set lower on the seat and slightly angled to give your seat a visual lift

TOSS
Jeans that:

- are overly embellished, especially with embroidery or sparkles

- have unintentional holes and/or tears

- are "Mommy"-style jeans or feature a gathered elastic waistband, which can look dated and age your overall look

- continue to bleed dye regardless of how many times they have been washed

- have a rise that is too high or too low for you to wear comfortably

- are faded

- are baggy

- expose unintended body parts

- create a muffin top

- are too tight to be comfortable

KEEP
Shorts and capris that:

- don't make you feel self-conscious when you bend over

- have an inseam that looks good with the length of your legs

- have a rise that feels good on you

TOSS
Shorts and capris that:

- are too short to be age appropriate

- have a zipper that does not function properly

- have a button fly that is difficult to work with

KEEP

These six skirts:

- pencil skirt, which works for a variety of occasions

- pleated skirt (when paired with a simple top, it looks professional)

- maxi skirt for casual outings

- denim skirt for when jeans are just not dressy enough

- casual A-line skirt

- hi-low skirt that is longer in the back for good leg coverage if you are self-conscious about the backs of your legs

TOSS

Skirts that:

- don't go with anything else in your wardrobe

- are so long you constantly trip on them and can't be hemmed

- are too constricting or too revealing

KEEP

Sweaters that:

- are versatile, especially a cardigan that pairs well with a dress, skirt, jeans, or dress pants

- have a comfortable neck that isn't too tight or too loose

- are an appropriate weight for your climate or preferred home temperature

TOSS

Sweaters that:

- are too pilled or moth-eaten

- are stretched out or misshapen, shrunken, or have hanger bumps

- irritate your skin, forcing you to add a layer underneath

KEEP

These tops:

- white button-down

- black tank top

- polo shirt in a neutral color, like navy, black, white, or beige

- short-sleeved T-shirts and three-quarter-sleeve tops in basic colors, like white and black

- long-sleeved T-shirts in neutral colors, like navy, white, black, and beige

- black turtleneck, which can easily be dressed up or down

- crewneck sweater in a thinner knit, which can be used for layering

- any tops you wear frequently because they fit well, are comfortable, and suit your style

TOSS
These tops:

- concert, volunteer, or free merchandise T-shirts you never wear (if you want to keep a few as memorabilia, see Chapter 13)

- anything with armpit stains that can't be washed out

- anything that is too form-fitting

- anything that gapes open or where the buttons strain, pop, or won't close

KEEP/TOSS CLUE: If you always get compliments on a sweater or top and feel great in it, keep it.

---

10 Unexpected Ways to Wear a White Button-Down Shirt

1. Under a short-sleeve or sleeveless dress
2. Over a short-sleeve or sleeveless dress
3. With a suit blazer and slacks
4. As a swimsuit cover-up
5. Tucked into a pencil skirt
6. With blue jeans
7. Over leggings/jeggings
8. With a scarf
9. Tied at the waist and with sleeves cuffed, paired with shorts
10. Paired with a wide belt and tall boots

KEEP

PJs and robes that are:

- pretty (ugly clothing doesn't make you feel good)

- stylish yet soft and comfortable

- the appropriate weight for your climate or preferred home temperature

- machine-washable

- resistant to pilling and lint trails

- pocketed, for carrying small essentials

- part of a sleep set you still like to wear

TOSS

PJs and robes that are:

- too wide or long in the arms so that they are a hazard while working in the kitchen

- detailed with scratchy buttons, lace, or clothing tags that can't be removed

- too tight or constricting

- made of unbreathable fabric that makes you sweat

- too heavy

- not machine- or hand-washable

- likely to pill or that get small holes easily

- stretched out and unflattering

KEEP/TOSS CLUE: No one says you have to own a robe. Sometimes what sounds luxurious is just an extra thing to figure out what to do with.

KEEP

Swimwear and cover-ups that:

- are a classic cut flattering to your figure

- are comfortable to wear without fear of slipping straps or coming untied

- are easy to slip on and off

- have pockets for carrying essentials (cover-ups only)

TOSS
Swimwear and cover-ups that:

- are stretched, faded, or stained

- are too revealing to wear without feeling self-conscious

- aren't easy to care for or are not machine-washable

> **KEEP/TOSS CLUE:** Your cover-up should be appropriate for how and when you use it. A sexy sarong might work in your own backyard, but for a day at the water park with children, you might want something with a little more coverage. When and where are you actually going to wear it?

KEEP
These five handbags:

- everyday: with multiple compartments for organization that works with almost every outfit and occasion (You may prefer to store this in your entryway; see Chapter 1.)

- casual clutch: you can toss it in your larger tote bag and just grab it to run into the store

- dressy clutch: perfect to carry your essentials for a night out

- weekend tote: an easy-to-clean material; throw everything in the bag for a day trip

- trendy bag: an easy way to introduce a new trend into your wardrobe; use it for a season or two

TOSS
Handbags that:

- were trendy but are no longer in style

- you no longer use

- you can never find anything in

- are too shiny or have too many embellishments or hardware to make them work for everyday use (unless you want to make it your dressy clutch)

KEEP

Socks, hosiery, and tights adding up to a total of 25 pairs per adult:

- 7 pairs of athletic/gym socks
- 7 pairs of dress/lightweight
- 4 pairs of thick wooly/fuzzy socks
- 2 pairs of panty hose
- 2 pairs of tights
- 1 pair of slipper socks
- add in 2 pairs of whatever you wear the most of between laundry cycles

TOSS

Toss socks, hosiery, and tights that:

- are stained or have holes
- fall down or are stretched out
- are too small or too tight
- are worn out
- are itchy or uncomfortable
- are slippery to walk in without shoes
- are holiday- or season-specific and you don't wear them
- are in colors and patterns you'd never wear or don't match outfits
- are missing their mates (socks)

KEEP/TOSS CLUE: If you have any orphaned socks, keep 4 or 5 of them with your cleaning supplies. They work well for dusting.

KEEP

Shoes that are:

- comfortable and don't pinch your toes or give you blisters

- safe to walk in

- flattering on your foot

- your style and taste

- appropriate for your current lifestyle and regular activities

TOSS

Shoes that are:

- broken beyond repair

- scuffed beyond polishing

- worn out in the sole or too worn down to revive

- ill-fitted (too tight, too narrow, or too big)

- prone to cause blisters

- dangerous to wear, such as those with a too-high heel or slippery soles—no shoe is worth risking a fall

- unsuitable for your lifestyle

- so outfit-specific they can hardly be worn

- too similar to other pairs you own

- hopelessly outdated

---

12 Shoes Every Woman Should Have in Her Closet

1. Ballet flats
2. Black pumps
3. Dress boots
4. Flip-flops
5. Sandals
6. Loafers
7. Seasonal or rain boots
8. Slippers
9. Tennis shoes/sneakers
10. Wedges
11. Heels to wear with your go-to little black dress
12. Inexpensive trendy shoes you keep for a season or two

KEEP THIS, TOSS THAT

Jewelry and Accessories

KEEP
Necklaces that:

- work with a variety of outfits

- fall at the right length for the necklines you wear most often

- you would buy again today

- match your current style

- match a specific outfit you love to wear

- stay in place when wearing

TOSS
Necklaces that:

- have broken pieces, such as a clasp that opens unexpectedly, that can't be repaired, or that you won't get around to fixing

- are oversized, trendy statement necklaces you have nothing to wear with or are simply out of style

- are broken costume pieces

- are fussy to wear, like a pendant that constantly flips or twists

- you are keeping out of guilt because they were gifts

- have chains that catch and pull your hair

- tarnish easily and are too time-consuming to maintain

KEEP
Earrings that:

- serve as a go-to everyday pair

- are good for a special occasion (studs are most versatile)

- work best with your hairstyle

TOSS
Earrings that:

- you don't have a match for

- irritate your ears

KEEP
Rings that:

- you really like and wear all the time

- fit the finger you prefer to wear it on

- are easy to clean

- are a preferable weight

TOSS
Rings that:

- are trendy or sit too high on your finger to be practical

- aren't comfortable to wear

- turn your finger green

- are too time-consuming to polish or care for

- are broken and not worth the repair cost

KEEP
Bracelets and wristwatches that:

- are your favorite go-to everyday pieces

- fit your style today

- wear easily and aren't fussy, like a bracelet that constantly flips

- allow air to circulate so you don't perspire underneath

TOSS
Bracelets and wristwatches that:

- are too tight or too loose and not able to be adjusted easily or inexpensively

- catch on or pull at your clothing

- just don't fit your style any longer

- have tarnished and are inexpensive

- are broken and not worth fixing

- cause itching or a rash when you wear it

- don't keep proper time (wristwatches)

KEEP
Belts that:

- flatter your body shape

- go with outfits you already own

- are in good condition or are easy to repair or clean

TOSS
Belts that:

- go with an outfit you no longer own

- do not fit your current waist size and can't be adjusted by adding new holes

- have worn-out or broken loops or holes and aren't worth the expense to repair

KEEP/TOSS CLUE: It's all right to keep jewelry from your childhood or that is too formal to wear regularly if you intend to make it a family heirloom. But if you don't have kids or your children don't have the same style as you, then pass it on to a beloved friend or relative or have it reworked into a new piece you love!

Chapter 7
Kids' Rooms

You and your kids have better things to do than spend all day trying to clean up a bedroom. If you can't see the floor underneath the layers of toys, then paring down is the answer.

Involving your children in the process helps them develop organizational skills. Sure, it might take longer to let them help choose the keepers and pick the tosses, but in the long run, working together this way gives little ones a lifelong skill. Opt for simple storage options, like bins without lids, so even toddlers can help you put toys inside.

Kids get new clothes and toys all the time, so to keep clutter under control, fill the box the new item came in with older ones to give away. Here's a little trade secret just between us: There may be times when some items need to "disappear" from your child's room when he or she is not around. Place the toys your child no longer plays with in a "maybe" box. If in the next six months your child asks for the toy, you can make it reappear. If not, you can donate without worry.

Ask yourself these key questions:

1. Is it something my child always avoids wearing, or doesn't want to wear, because of the material, design, color, or other reason?
2. Is the item way below their suggested age range?
3. Has their interest in the item faded?

There are some items you may want to hold on to for sentimental reasons. The "regular" keep/toss rules do not apply to these keepsakes, which is why I dedicated an entire chapter to treasures (see Chapter 13). For the rest, let's start tossing so you can put an end to those dreaded all-day cleanups once and for all!

Toys and Games

KEEP

Action figures and playsets that:

- are in good condition

- stand up and are easy to play with

- are easy to grab and pack for travel

TOSS

Action figures and playsets that:

- have missing limbs and heads

- are rarely played with

- have missing accessories

- are broken

KEEP

Blocks and building sets that:

- fit neatly in your storage space

- are different enough from one another to justify having them all

TOSS

Blocks and building sets that:

- your child doesn't play with

- have too many pieces, making storage difficult

- don't fit together easily or stay connected

- cause damage, like real wood blocks that dent your floors when they fall

KEEP

These arts and crafts items:

- kits that have everything still intact, such as looms, beads, and stained-glass art

- stamp kits with fresh ink

- stickers that are still sticky

TOSS

These arts and crafts items:

- anything that is too messy to be enjoyable (for you or your child) for fear of staining or damaging clothing or your home

- paints that are almost used up

- crayon stubs or those broken into bits

- markers that are missing caps or dried up

- crumpled construction or drawing paper

- bent, torn, or mostly used-up sketchbooks

- seen-better-days art supplies, like ragged paint brushes

- hardened or crumbly clay or dough

STORAGE SOLUTION

Put games and craft sets that require adult supervision, like pottery, beading, or race-car kits, in a closet or on a shelf away from little fingers. When you hear your child utter the dreaded phrase "I'm bored," just pull one out to enjoy together.

KEEP

These games and toys that are appropriate for your kids' ages, skill levels, and interests:

- 12 board and/or card games that your family plays together and are in good condition

- 10 stuffed animals

- 3 dolls with accessories

- 3 puzzles per age level per child you haven't assembled yet but will in the next six months

- 2 building sets and blocks

- 2 coloring books per child

- 1 activity book per skill level per child

- handheld electronic games that are still enjoyed

TOSS

Children's games and toys that:

- have been long ignored

- are expensive to maintain (for instance, a game that uses lots of batteries quickly)

- are bulky space stealers, like play kitchens, that are rarely (if ever) used

- are a choking or electrical hazard

- are duplicates or different versions of the same game (like three versions of Monopoly)

- are broken, flimsy, frustrating, or don't work properly

- can't be cleaned

- have too many pieces to keep track of

- are missing instructions, parts, or pieces that you have no hope of recovering

- are too difficult or time-consuming to play

Did you know?

It can be helpful to box up and store the small plastic toys from goodie bags and drive-thru meals to use in future school projects, like three-dimensional dioramas.

KEEP
These baby and toddler toys:

- teethers and rattles that are in good condition and are still used

- stacking toys that have all their pieces

TOSS
These baby and toddler toys:

- tub toys that are mildewed

- anything of which you have an excessive amount

KEEP
Inside walk and ride-on toys that:

- are still fun and played with

- your child still fits on or in

- are easy to play with

- have a long battery life

TOSS
Inside walk and ride-on toys that:

- are just too large for your home

- are dangerous because they roll too quickly, causing possible injury

- are too similar to other toys you're keeping

- are too loud to be enjoyable to play with (for you or your children)

KEEP
Activity mats that:

- your child still enjoys playing on

- have all the pieces securely attached

TOSS
Activity mats that:

- your child has outgrown

- are dirty but not machine-washable

KEEP

Dolls and accessories that:

- still have all their limbs

- are still fun to play with

- are loved and cared for

TOSS

Dolls and accessories that:

- have matted or cut-off hair

- your child has outgrown

- are too similar to dolls you're already keeping

- are just in excess

> ### STORAGE SOLUTION
> ....
> Designate an area in the home to display your child's artwork and completed projects, like potholders and sun catchers. As new items come into this "gallery," older items are tossed. If they are keepsake-worthy, they get a space in your child's treasure box for safe-keeping.

KEEP

These items for dress-up and pretend play:

- costumes that have all their pieces

- hats that are not crushed

- wigs, jewelry, or other accessories that are still in good condition

TOSS

These items for dress-up and pretend play:

- high-heeled shoes that are a trip-and-fall danger

- damaged crowns with missing gemstones

- cracked masks

- masks that are dangerous to wear because they make it difficult to breathe or see

KEEP
Toy musical instruments that are:

- easy to play

- clean and easy to clean

- intact with all keys, buttons, strings, etc.

TOSS
Toy musical instruments that:

- don't have volume-control options

- are dangerous to use and could cause injury

- are often used incorrectly, like to bang on other things

KEEP
These stuffed animals and plush toys:

- teddy bears that are still loved

- plush backpacks and purses that have working zippers

TOSS
Stuffed animals and plush toys that:

- have no hope of getting cleaned

- are no longer played with

KEEP
Balls and indoor sports equipment that:

- are soft, such as small balls intended for indoor play

- are still fun to play with

- are part of a game and all pieces are intact

TOSS
Balls and indoor sports equipment that:

- are too large to use inside

- are deflated or partially deflated

- are dangerous to use inside for fear of breaking something

KEEP

Toy remote control, play vehicles, and train sets that:

- are still fun to play with

- set up fast enough that the child doesn't lose interest in playing

- are easy to clean up

TOSS

Toy remote control, play vehicles, and train sets that:

- are missing remotes

- drain batteries too quickly

- are rechargeable but missing the charger

- have an antenna that is damaged beyond repair

- are too large to store

KEEP/TOSS CLUE: If a collection has gotten too large, you can pare down the pieces instead of tossing the whole set.

KEEP

Household replicas and pop-ups that:

- are still in use and in good repair

- are easy to fold and store away

- stay up and are fun to use

- are good quality and function as intended

TOSS

Household replicas and pop-ups that:

- are only played with when you perform the activity (such as a toy vacuum cleaner that is only played with when you vacuum)

- are oversized, with bulky plastic pieces you don't have room to store

- are not played with

- are lopsided and easily tip over

Books

KEEP
About 30 children's books that:

- you read and reread to your children

- are good stories with messages you believe in

- are written by authors you love

- still hold your child's interest

- are at or above your child's current reading level

- are signed by the author or illustrator

TOSS
Children's books that:

- are below your child's reading level

- are too torn to read or are otherwise damaged

- have characters you do not want to expose your children to

- you will not reread

- have characters, drawings, or stories that frighten or upset your child

- have noise built in that is distracting

- contain topics your children are no longer interested in

- are duplicates (or triplicates) of the same book

- are used-up coloring or activity books

- are e-books that were read but will not be reread

- are e-books that will never be read

Furniture and Decor

KEEP

These pieces of kids' furniture and storage solutions:

- bed

- bookshelf

- bedside table

- a double hang bar in the closet to double the hanging space available in the closet, while bringing hanging clothes lower for little hands to grab independently

- baskets or storage bins with labels or photos so the contents can be identified at a glance, and without the lids (unless the boxes must be stacked), because lids prevent organization by requiring that extra step to take the lid off just to put something away

- toy trolleys on wheels

- any storage option that is currently working well (you may consider adding even more of the same style)

TOSS

These pieces of kids' furniture and storage solutions:

- dresser, if you have enough closet space to hang clothing and shelves in the closet for folded items

- dirty clothes hamper that is too small to hold the laundry

- toy chests

- unused or excess furniture, like an unused bean bag chair, or pieces that are simply too large to fit in the space

- storage containers that are too small to effectively store anything

KEEP

These pieces of decor:

- alarm clock

- pillows

- tabletop night lamp

- motion-activated nightlight that plugs into an outlet (if age appropriate)

- piggy bank

- framed photographs

- decorative items on display

TOSS

These pieces of decor:

- unreliable alarm clocks

- broken piggy banks that can't be repaired

- more than three decorative pillows

KEEP/TOSS CLUE: To avoid cluttering the room with completed crafts and other projects, awards, and trophies, consider designating one shelf for each. When the shelf is full, it is time to make some keep/toss decisions.

STORAGE SOLUTION

Limit projects still in progress, like a spaceship being built out of small brick blocks, to one small tabletop, tray, or basket. This allows the project to continue, but it avoids projects taking over every horizontal space in the room.

Clothing

KEEP

Infant clothing that:

- still fits your child

- is easy to get on and off

- stays put and stays on

- isn't irritating to the skin

- you still think is cute

TOSS

Infant clothing that is:

- stained beyond cleaning

- not a style you like seeing your child in

- too fancy for everyday wear

- too small

KEEP

Toddler and preschooler clothing that is:

- part of your child's favorite outfits

- in your child's favorite colors

- easy to put on and take off

- necessary for a particular activity

TOSS

Toddler and preschooler clothing that is:

- stained

- torn or has holes in it

- uncomfortable to wear

- too small

16 Diaper-Bag Essentials

1. Diapers
2. Baby wipes
3. Diaper cream
4. Changing pad
5. Clothing for your baby
6. Baby socks
7. Burp cloths
8. Bibs
9. Blanket
10. One or two small toys
11. Baby bottle
12. Baby food and feeding supplies
13. Tissues
14. Nursing pads
15. Water bottle
16. An extra change of clothes for you

KEEP
School-age children's clothing that:

- is part of your child's favorite go-to outfits

- is age appropriate

- has a hemline that is still appropriate on your growing child

- has an extendable waistband that will grow with your child

- is needed for a particular activity

TOSS
School-age children's clothing that:

- no longer fits your child

- your child never wears

- is itchy or scratchy

- is immodest or otherwise inappropriate

- keeps coming undone

- is no longer stylish or age appropriate

- is for activities your child is no longer involved with

Did you know?

If you have children under age 15, you should keep child-size hangers.
Larger, adult-size hangers may stretch out children's clothes.

KEEP
Shoes that:

- go with multiple outfits

- your child likes to wear

- are comfortable

- are easy to put on and take off

TOSS
Shoes that:

- are too worn out to be safe

- have broken backs

- are too small for your child

- are always slipping off

- have lace holes that are stretched out of shape or torn

- won't stay tied or strapped closed

- cause blisters or are uncomfortable

STORAGE SOLUTION

Set boundaries to keep clutter in check. Designate a specific amount of space for certain items. Once a space is filled, you must toss some to make room. For example, if you have a shoe organizer that fits a dozen pairs of shoes, then when you get a thirteenth pair, you must toss one.

Chapter 8
Storage Spaces, Garage, and Car

If you have an attic, basement, bonus room, or other similar space in your house, chances are it's become a dumping ground for all the stuff you haven't had the time or energy to tidy up. While it's perfectly natural to use these spaces for storage, try not to store things there just because you can. Ideally, you want to know exactly what you have stored there and be able to easily access it when you want it.

Similarly, if you have to park your car in the driveway because your garage is too cluttered, then it's time to take back this misused space. Just a few tosses can result in a big payoff since many of the items hanging out here are large, so letting them go means getting back a lot of space quickly.

Remember, these spaces are usually not climate-controlled; therefore, they are prone to overheating, excessive coldness, dampness, and humid conditions. So it can actually be destructive to stash things there.

While we're making space to get the car parked inside the garage, we'll also address what you need to keep and toss from your car. Evaluate what you realistically need to have on hand. If your car is a mobile office, then you'll need to keep a box of business cards and lots of extra pens. But if you shuffle three children to and from a variety of sports practices every week, you probably need to clean out some food and candy wrappers.

Ask yourself these key questions:
1. Can I rent this or borrow the item from a friend or neighbor?
2. Can I afford to give up the space this takes to store?
3. Can I hire someone who will bring their own tools or supplies (like a lawn-mower) to do the job?

It's time to take back the space so you can finally park your newly organized car in your newly cleared garage!

In the Attic and Basement

KEEP

Items you use seasonally such as decorations

- Out-of-season clothing that you'll wear again next year

- Activity and outing gear and accessories like a cooler

- Keepsakes that have already been sorted and are now well packed

- Product boxes for items that are still under warranty (in case you need to return or exchange the item)

TOSS

Old, duplicate, or broken decor and furnishings

- Broken, chipped, cracked, or unused glassware, table ware, or vases

- Old appliances, furniture, curtains, lamps, and lampshades

- Project pieces like a chair you planned to reupholster

- Empty boxes

- Boxes of belongings never opened from previous moves

- Mailing supplies such as boxes, bubble wrap, or packing pillows

- Hand-me-downs that you never needed or used or that don't suit your taste or style

In the Garage

KEEP
These car-cleaning products:

- exterior and interior cleaners that work for your car

- windshield cleaner

- tire and rim cleaner

- all-purpose cleaner for interior plastics, vinyl, leather, rubber, and metal

- lint-free, absorbent towels

TOSS
Car cleaners that:

- are streaky or leave the surface sticky

- are crumbly and dried out

- are difficult to apply or buff off

- leave residue or lint behind

KEEP
These five car-care tools:

- wheel brush

- bucket, 3 gallons or larger

- vent and dash brush

- crevice tool

- brake-dust remover brush

TOSS
These car-care tools:

- tiny detailing tools that don't work well

- power washers that are too harsh for the car's surface

- battery-operated buffers or wax machines that are difficult to operate

- car-care accessories that attach to your drill but are more trouble than they're worth

KEEP

These handy tools:

- level

- 12-volt cordless drill

- assorted fasteners (nuts, bolts, washers, anchors, and nails in various sizes)

- plumbers' tape

- duct tape

- can of WD-40

- pliers

- needle-nose pliers

- one short-handled and one long-handled Phillips screwdriver

- one short-handled and one long-handled flat-head screwdriver

- clawed hammer

- box cutter with a retractable blade

- silicone tape

- Loctite or Gorilla glue (a "super" glue that works on most surfaces)

TOSS

These workbench items and tools:

- tape measures less than 1" wide, which makes them floppy when extended

- wrench set (just keep one adjustable wrench)

- any excess tools or tools you don't use

- dented, leaking, or rusty cans of oil or chemicals or cans missing an applicator (like a straw)

- leftover parts from projects, like a tube of glue that is mostly dried up

- cans and samples of paint that are dried out or in colors you won't use anymore

- rusted equipment, nails, and screws

- random pieces for woodworking and scraps of wood

- half-completed woodworking projects

- excess Allen wrenches from self-assembly furniture

- leftover wallpaper

- spare tiles

7 Items That Should Never Be Stored in Your Garage

1. Paper—as in paperwork, books, or paper goods, like paper towels

2. Photographs and other memorabilia

3. Fabrics that are likely to develop mildew and musty smells

4. Items in cardboard boxes, such as boxed food

5. Metals that are prone to rusting, such as fishing gear and metal toolboxes

6. Collectibles, like vinyl records, which can warp

7. Propane tanks for your gas grill (these are better kept outside where it's well-ventilated to prevent igniting the fumes when you start your car)

KEEP

These seasonally themed decorations:

- light strands that work

- your favorite door wreath or sign (one for each season)

- Easter eggs that are still colorful

- scarecrow, oversized cornucopia, and ornamental corn in good condition

- artificial Christmas tree and decorations that are used year after year

TOSS

Seasonally themed decorations that:

- are crushed, crumbling, cracked, rusted, dented, musty, and/or falling apart

- are broken beyond repair, or you will not take the time to repair

- are faded and have seen better days

- are torn or won't stay inflated

- are missing pieces

- you no longer enjoy looking at or you avoid putting up/out, for whatever reason, year after year

KEEP

Boxes and electronics packaging that:

- are for large electronics that you plan to sell in the next year

- are for electronics you're keeping if you plan to move in the next year and it is easier to transport the item in original packaging

- are for small tech items that get better resale with the box and are upgraded regularly (includes: smartphones, digital cameras, and laptops)

- are collectible, but only if you plan to sell it

KEEP/TOSS CLUE: If you are going to keep the box, take a photo of how items were packed originally before removing elements. This will make repacking easier if you move or plan to resell items. Be sure to write the expiration date of the item's manufacturer's warranty coverage, if applicable.

TOSS

Boxes and electronics packaging that:

- are for items you are keeping and plan to use for more than two years

- are from large appliances, as long as you've been using the appliance for a few weeks and are sure it's in working condition

- are simply filler, such as packing peanuts, air pillows, bubble wrap, and Styrofoam packing blocks

- are for products you no longer own

- are for items you've held past the return/exchange date and are not under warranty

- don't hold up or have gotten damp

- won't fit in proper storage (garage critters tend to nest in them)

Did you know?

Most pack-and-ship locations will accept used packing peanuts, bubble wrap, and air pillows.

KEEP/TOSS CLUE: For home inventory and insurance purposes take a photo of a product box before you toss it. The box will have all the information, like brand and model. Then recycle the box discretely instead of leaving it curbside for unknown passersby to note what shiny new items are residing in your home.

KEEP
Trash and recycling cans that:

- have lids to keep pests out

- are large enough to accommodate your trash and recycling

- have easy-maneuver wheels to get up and over the curb

TOSS
Trash and recycling cans that:

- no longer roll

- are cracked or broken

- are too worn out to be useful

Did you know?

Most hazardous-waste collections will not accept tires, but most local tire retailers will accept your old tire for recycling. Some may charge a small fee.

8 Hazardous Items Not Typically Accepted in Trash/Recycling Pick-Up

1. Ammunition
2. Asbestos
3. Biological waste
4. Commercial waste
5. High-pressure cylinders (acetylene, oxygen, air tanks)
6. Radioactive materials
7. Explosives
8. Tires

In the Car

KEEP

These items inside the car:

- mini first-aid kit
- working flashlight
- spare phone charger
- extra sunglasses
- twenty-dollar bill
- nail clippers with attached file
- napkins or paper towels
- clean set of clothes
- window shades to block out the sun

Include these items if you have children:

- clean set of clothes for each child
- games
- sunglasses (for the kids)

TOSS

These items from inside the car:

- empty food wrappers and used napkins
- leftover, crushed snacks
- old receipts
- pens without ink
- recycling or donations you've been planning to drop off
- broken sunglasses
- corroded jumper cables
- half-empty cans of WD-40
- half-used bottles of engine oil
- flashlights with burned out lightbulbs
- first-aid kits that are missing essentials

Cold-Weather Car Gear

If you live in a cold-weather climate, keep these items in your car during the winter (and in your garage during the warmer seasons):

- collapsible shovel

- ice scraper

- lock de-icer

- snow brush

- portable air compressor to reinflate tires

- small pieces of carpet for traction under tires in snow

- spare blanket

- tow strap

- 2 quarts of oil for the car

KEEP/TOSS CLUE: Conduct a keep/toss session seasonally to toss items from your car that you won't need for another year, like an ice scraper in June, which you can store outside the car until you need it again.

KEEP

These items In your car or in the trunk, as you have space, if you venture out on daylong, or longer, road trips:

- change for vending machines
- comfortable shoes in case you need to walk a long distance
- a cooler
- nonperishable food and drinks
- frisbee or other sports to play at rest stops
- matches and/or a lighter (stored properly away from children)
- one gallon of clean water per person
- paper map
- pillow
- toilet paper (sometimes rest stops run out)
- trash bag
- 2 quarts of oil for the car
- windshield cleaner with a rag
- spare pair of eyeglasses (if you wear them)
- over-the-counter medication for headache and stomach upset

Include these pet-friendly items if you travel with your dog:

- treats and two servings of dog food
- extra leash
- your veterinarian's phone number
- phone number to a local vet near where you are traveling
- phone number to a pet-friendly hotel where you are traveling
- 1 toy
- waste bags
- water and water bowl

KEEP/TOSS CLUE: Keep your dog's ID tag and license clipped directly to his/her collar in the unlikely event you are separated.

Your Roadside Emergency Kit

Before you stow away your roadside emergency kit, check to be sure you have a fully inflated spare tire, a jack, a lug wrench, and jumper cables in your trunk or a fully charged portable jump-starter box. Then make a kit with the following items and keep it in your trunk at all times:

- adjustable wrench
- duct tape
- fire extinguisher
- first-aid kit
- flashlight and extra batteries
- flat-head screwdriver
- fuse kit

- gloves
- paper towels
- Phillips screwdriver
- plastic, stand-up, reflective warning triangles
- pliers
- pocketknife

- rags
- shovel (folding or compact)
- tire inflator
- tire pressure gauge
- vise grips
- waterproof vinyl HELP sign to hang on car

KEEP/TOSS CLUE: Your car can easily become a storage unit on wheels, complete with bags of donations you meant to drop off and dry cleaning you picked up but never brought in the house. Toss this stuff out of the car by following through on the task.

Chapter 9
Outdoor Spaces

Outdoor space is an extension of your home, a place to get outside and enjoy nature. Whether you look forward to dinner under the stars, love gardening, lounging by the pool, entertaining on the deck, or reading a book on the patio, you want the space to be enjoyable and clutter-free.

While at one time you may have been a master gardener, maybe you've since simplified to a much smaller, potted garden—which means you can toss all those unneeded supplies. Did your last home have landscaping services that you are now responsible for? If so, then you need to keep more equipment than someone who still has landscaping help.

No matter how much (or how little) outdoor space you have, the goal is to keep the proper tools and accessories on hand so it is easy to maintain and enjoy! And to be realistic about how you use your space, so you have room to store those tools you need.

Ask yourself these key questions:

1. Is it in good condition?
2. Does it make me happy or unhappy to see it?
3. Is it a leftover from a past growing season that I won't use again?

If you've been stockpiling items for maintaining those gorgeous gardens you plotted out five years ago but are never going to have the time or budget to create, it's time to weed your toolshed.

Balcony, Porch, and Patio Items

KEEP

Lawn or patio furniture that is:

- in good repair

- comfortable to use

- easy to rinse off

- completely water- and weather-proof

- adjustable, such as a chair that offers multiple settings

Also be sure to keep:

- a sun umbrella that opens fully, is large enough to cover the area needed, and folds down easily

- an outdoor rug that is in good repair and works with your space

TOSS

Lawn or patio furniture that is:

- ripped, torn, or missing pieces

- flimsy, weak, or rusted

- too wobbly, unstable, or otherwise dangerous to actually sit on

- too small to be useful, like an outgrown child-size chair

- too low to the ground and difficult to get in and out of

- not made from a water-repellent fabric, so it holds moisture and stays wet for hours

- bent or broken

- musty or mildewed

Also be sure to toss:

- cushions that no longer fit furniture sizes you own

- sun umbrellas that are not weighted, meaning they could tip over

- outdoor rugs that are faded, torn, or fraying or that lift up on the edges, making them a tripping hazard

Outdoor Accessories

KEEP
Fountains and water features that:

- consistently work well

- are sturdy and not a tipping hazard

- run and drain well

- have all the pieces

TOSS
Fountains and water features that:

- are broken and not cost effective to replace

- have tubing that continually clogs

- are too time-consuming to maintain properly

- have a noisy pump that drowns out the soothing sound of flowing water

- are algae-laden

- are electrical hazards with fraying wires

- evaporate quickly, meaning you have to refill it too often

- are bug and mosquito breeding grounds

- are not heavy enough to withstand a gusty wind

- are missing pieces and can't be assembled properly

- you're just tired of having around

- plug in and add too much to your monthly electric bill

- are solar-powered and don't get enough sunlight to fully charge

Garden sculptures and statues that are:

- weather-proof

- something that you still like looking at

- representative of your style

- in good repair

TOSS

Garden sculptures and statues that are:

- cracked, chipped, or broken

- faded in color, tired, or worn out

- you no longer love

- missing pieces

- lightweight so that they can turn into flying projectiles in strong winds

KEEP

Wind sculptures, chimes, and lights that:

- are in good repair

- still move well in the breeze

- you love to listen to (chimes)

- are café-style lights on strings

- are easy-to-assemble, solar-powered lights that still hold a charge

- use solar-powered batteries that are easy to replace (lights)

TOSS

Wind sculptures, chimes, and lights that:

- are cracked, rusted, or otherwise broken beyond repair

- are missing strands or pieces

- are too tangled to ever work well again

- you've grown tired of hearing (chimes)

- cannot withstand high winds or a strong storm

- have compromised wires

- have broken or unstable stakes

- are motion-activated and no longer detect motion or turn on (lights)

- do not hold a charge or stay lit (lights)

- have a plastic housing that has become hazy or cloudy (lights)

- are bug lights that do not actually deter pests

KEEP

These yard accents, plaques, and accessories:

- house numbers that are easily noticed from the road

- a welcome mat that looks inviting

- citronella candles with enough left in them to burn

- a weather-resistant clock

- a weather gauge or thermometer that tells the accurate temperature

- birdfeeders that fill easily

- hummingbird nectar holders that are simple to fill and easy to rinse out

TOSS

These yard accents, plaques, and accessories:

- house numbers that are not easily spotted or read from the road

- welcome mats that are shedding, falling apart, or hopelessly faded

- welcome mats that do not do their job of catching dirt and debris from shoe bottoms

- bug catchers that are filled and can't be cleaned out

- broken birdfeeders

- outdoor clocks that do not keep the correct time

- cracked planters and urns

KEEP
Flags, flagpoles, and garden flags that:

- you still like

- are sturdy and in good repair

- have all their pieces and are easy to assemble

- are seasonal house flags, celebration or occasion flags, or flags for sporting teams you root for, and that you actually take the time to put up

TOSS
Flags, flagpoles, and garden flags that:

- fit pole sizes you no longer own

- are faded, torn, or fraying

- are bent, rusted, or are missing pieces, making them unusable

- are for occasions you do not celebrate

- are American flags you aren't able to light properly or take down at night

Did you know?

Proper care and display of the American flag is dictated by federal code, and in some areas of the United States, there are penalties for flying the national flag at night without proper illumination. Find out the rules in your city, county, and state to avoid fines.

STORAGE SOLUTION

To prevent creasing, roll smaller garden flags and tuck them into the pockets of an over-the-door shoe organizer that you can hang on the garage wall or the back of the garage door.

KEEP THIS, TOSS THAT

Gardening and Landscaping Supplies

KEEP
Garden shears that:

- are heavy-duty

- have comfortable or ergonomic handles

- are sharp enough to get the job done

- have a small point for precise cutting

TOSS
Garden shears that:

- are difficult to maneuver with gardening gloves on

- give you blisters after prolonged use

- will not open and close smoothly

- are rusted or otherwise damaged

KEEP
A weeder that is:

- narrow enough to reach down to roots

- sharp enough to cut roots

- fitted with a cushioned grip

- sturdy for working in solid soil

TOSS
Weeders that are:

- bent or will bend easily

- cheap, inexpensive, or poorly made

- less than 12" long, rendering them less useful

- uncomfortable to handle

Did you know?

If you need to trim branches more than 1" in diameter,
you'll probably need a pruning saw to get the job done.

Pruning shears that are:

- lightweight, for extended use

- comfortable to hold

- easy to compress

- sharp and have bypass blades for easy cutting

- ideal for stems and light branches

- fitted with a locking closure to prevent accidents

TOSS

Pruning shears that are:

- so sap-covered that they are ineffective

- hard to snip even thin branches with

- rusted or broken in any way

- difficult to handle with gardening gloves on

KEEP

Snips that are:

- spring-loaded for rapid, light clipping, like deadheading rose bushes

- fitted with a soft-grip, ergonomic handle for easy, extended use

- narrow for precision cutting of fruit and flower stems

TOSS

Snips that are:

- too heavy to use for an extended period

- not stainless steel or corrosion-resistant

- don't lock because the locking clasp is missing or broken

Did you know?

Snips with a 4" handle
are the most versatile.

KEEP
These three gardening rakes:

- large yard rake with flexible tines to gather debris

- mini hand rake for turning small patches or clearing shallow weeds

- large, flat fan with sturdy tines for smoothing soil or mulch when used tine side up

TOSS
Rakes that are:

- prone to causing backaches when used for extended periods

- broken or cracked

- rough-handled or have splinters

- too small to get larger jobs done quickly

KEEP
Garden and plant markers that are:

- large enough to read

- durable to be out in the weather

- plastic so they won't rust

TOSS
Garden and plant markers that are:

- in excess of what you'll ever need

- rusted, bent, or so small they get lost

- so worn that you can no longer read the labels

- broken or cracked

KEEP/TOSS CLUE: Keeping a gardening "journal" is a helpful way to track the goings-on in your garden. Keep it simple by journaling on a wall calendar. Hang one along with a pen so you can jot notes as to when you planted and harvested, along with other important reminders.

KEEP

A watering can that:

- has a rotating spout for convenient pouring

- is made of plastic so it is lightweight for easy pouring without straining your arms

- has a nonslip handle for secure carrying

- is sized to carry water for a plant or two, but not so large that it's too heavy to lug

TOSS

Watering cans that:

- are small-capacity, which means unnecessary trips

- have sprung a leak

- are poorly designed and uncomfortable to use

- drip and get water where you don't want it

KEEP

Sprinklers that:

- give you the best coverage without much waste, based on the area you need to water

- oscillate to get more coverage

- are narrow or adjustable to better direct water

- are designed for concentrated spraying, to conserve water

TOSS

Sprinklers that:

- have clogged holes so water does not dispense

- have a broken oscillating feature so that it no longer functions properly

- do not offer multiple settings for a variety of spraying patterns

KEEP

Two gardening hats that:

- have an angled brim for longer, all-day protection as the sun rises and sets

- are comfortable and cool

- have a sweatband to keep sweat from dripping down your forehead

TOSS

Gardening hats that:

- have less than a 3" brim, offering little sun protection

- don't have a hoop-and-loop closure or neck cinch to prevent the hat from blowing off your head

- are hot to wear because the fabric is not vented

- are faded from the sun

- you just don't like wearing for whatever reason

KEEP

These gardening gloves:

- puncture-resistant with a knuckle guard for thorny plants and tough jobs

- elbow-length, coated gloves to protect forearms from cuts and scratches

- leather or cotton gloves to avoid blisters with heavy or repetitive jobs

- latex or rubber gloves to keep your hands dry while planting and weeding

TOSS

Gardening gloves that:

- are not shirred at the wrist so they keep slipping off

- are not your size

- you don't like the style, look, or feel of

- have little to no dexterity, making it difficult to complete tasks

- have holes or tears

- are uncomfortable

- don't offer a nonslip grip

- don't have a mate

11 Tools to Keep If You Maintain Your Own Landscaping

1. Chain saw for cutting tree limbs
2. Electric hedge trimmers for trimming bushes
3. Flat border spade to edge beds
4. Lawnmower
5. Leaf blower
6. Pruning saw
7. Rake
8. Saw
9. Tarp
10. Weedwacker
11. Wheelbarrow

KEEP/TOSS CLUE: Many tools can be rented from your local home-improvement store or borrowed from a neighbor. You do not have to purchase and then store every tool or piece of equipment, especially those you're only going to use once or twice a year.

Pool

KEEP
These pool-maintenance supplies:

- skimmer

- test kit

- wall and floor scrubber

- chemicals that are within date

TOSS
These pool-maintenance supplies:

- cleaning tools that do not do the job or are broken

- test kits without clear directions on how to use them

- chemicals that you no longer need or whose containers have rusted

KEEP
Pool toys that:

- have all the pieces and are in good condition

- are age-appropriate for your family

- you have the space to store

TOSS
Pool toys that:

- could cause injury or drowning

- are blow-up toys that no longer hold air

- are mildewed or musty and cannot be cleaned well

Did you know?

You shouldn't toss pool chemicals in the trash where
children or pets may be able to reach them.
You may be able to donate unneeded pool chemicals to your community pool. If not,
contact a local pool-supply store to ask if they accept chemicals for disposal, or bring
them to the next community hazardous waste cleanup day.

Chapter 10
Outings

If a fun outing turns stressful because you can't find the cooler, you might need to declutter. While you want to be prepared for an impromptu trip to listen to an outdoor concert at the park, you don't need to keep enough lawn chairs to seat half the neighborhood. And yes, you need luggage, but you can toss the suitcase with the broken handle.

If you have been collecting supplies for the beach vacation you never took or the overseas adventure you've been saving for, now is the time to make your dream of those "someday" trips into a reality. Take a moment now to pencil those trips into your calendar. Once they're scheduled, there is a much better chance you'll follow through with them.

Whether you are heading out by yourself, making it a girls' trip, or taking the kids with you, when the time comes to pack, you'll be organized and have all your supplies ready to go!

Ask yourself these key questions:

1. Do I have a particular use for this within the next year?
2. Does it have all the necessary pieces and parts?
3. What is the worst possible thing that could happen if I got rid of it?

Let's get going!

Sightseeing/Vacation

KEEP

Two pieces of luggage per family member that:

- have multidirectional, smooth-rolling wheels that spin 360°, making them very easy to maneuver

- have wheels that roll over a variety of surfaces

- have durable, easy-glide zippers

- include telescoping handles

- have compression straps on the inside to prevent contents from shifting

- have waterproof linings to keep spilled liquids from dripping out or from leaking in

- are made of a quick-dry fabric in case they do get wet

- have all the buckles and straps accounted for and easy to use

- are comfortable to walk with

- stand independently without tipping, even when full

- have the potential to expand by unzipping another small section

- have easy-to-access compartments and pockets

- won't easily damage when scraped

- offer roomy interiors

KEEP/TOSS CLUE: Check the weight of the bag when empty. Some bags weigh over 12 pounds before you put a thing inside! Since you have a 50- to 70-pound limit on checked luggage when you are flying (depending on your fare class), you don't want to waste a pound on heavy luggage. The average weight of a piece of luggage is 7.5 pounds when empty. Keep the lightest options.

TOSS

Luggage that:

- is broken and beyond the warranty-coverage period

- is old and full of tears and holes

- has wheels that are broken or stuck

- has a broken telescoping handle

- doesn't fit the kind of travel you do

- is hard-sided, which can crack or split and doesn't allow for expansion

- has odors or stains that can't be removed

Did you know?

When flying, if you lock your bag's main compartment and side pockets, which you should, it is recommended you use Transportation Safety Authority–compliant locks, which TSA screeners can open if they choose to search your bag. Otherwise, they will cut the locks, and you'll have to purchase new ones.

KEEP/TOSS CLUE: If you fly, keep bags that fit the carry-on size requirements. Check with your airline, but most allow you to carry on one bag (up to 22" x 14" x 9") and a personal item (up to 17" x 9" x 10"). Keep in mind: The dimensions include the handles and wheels.

KEEP

A travel alarm that:

- includes a battery backup to ensure you wake up even if the power fails

- is small and easy to pack

- is sturdy enough to withstand some knocking around

- has a pleasant alarm sound

TOSS

A travel alarm that:

- is unreliable

- is fragile or already broken

- is too soft a tone to wake you up

- is heavy or awkward to pack

One of the most commonly forgotten items when traveling overseas is a voltage converter. If you travel internationally, get one and store it inside your luggage.

KEEP

Guidebooks that:

- are the current editions for places you plan to visit in the next year

- cover the sights you want to see

- are small and light, if you plan on taking them along on the trip

TOSS

Guidebooks that:

- are two years old or older (the information and reviews have most likely changed)

- have information that would be better obtained "up to the minute," such as directions or current traveler reviews, which you can get online

- can be borrowed from the library or a friend or family member

STORAGE SOLUTION

If you don't travel very often, consider storing out-of-season clothing in your luggage. If you take a trip, you can just leave the clothing on the bed until you return.

Day Trips

KEEP

These items together for trips to amusement parks, the zoo, or museums:

- coins for lockers

- membership cards, season passes, entrance passes, venue discount coupons

- sunscreen and/or hats (for outdoor activities)

- zip-top bags—to put electronics (phone, camera) in if going on a wet ride or to keep wet clothing from getting other items in your bag wet

- straps for sunglasses or eyeglasses (so they don't fly off on rides)

- lightweight backpack or other small bag for keeping items with you

- change of clothes, if going on a wet ride

TOSS

These items from past trips to amusement parks, the zoo, or museums:

- expired membership cards, season passes, entrance passes, maps, brochures, or venue discount coupons

- refillable cups and other promotional gear that get you a discount for places you won't likely return to before the promotion ends, which might be at the end of the season

KEEP

These items for when you hit the stadium:

- a mitt to catch foul balls

- binoculars

- blanket for chilly nights

- stadium seat cushion (one for each family member) for when you have bleacher seats

- autograph book

- team hat or jersey

TOSS

These stadium supplies:

- chair cushions that are too flat to add comfort

- ragged or torn foam fingers and other game-time accessories

KEEP/TOSS CLUE: If you must buy souvenirs from your trip, consider clutter-free ones. Opt for something you need and that is useful, like a photo frame or a kitchen towel versus a plush toy.

Beach/Lake/Pool/Picnic

KEEP

One folding lawn chair per family member that:

- has a convenient cup holder

- comes with or can adapt to use an added sun umbrella for shade

- has a carrying strap for hands-free portability

- is in good working order

- is clean and mildew-free

- opens and closes easily

TOSS

Excess folding lawn chairs that:

- are broken or rusted

- are too heavy to carry a long distance comfortably

- tip easily or are otherwise unstable

- are so lightweight they are at risk of blowing away if not secured

- are uncomfortable to sit in

- have material that is worn out or fraying

KEEP/TOSS CLUE: In addition to lawn chairs for your family, keep four extras for guests. If you need more, then ask guests to bring their own. And remember, not everyone sits down in a lawn chair at the same time, and you may have other seating options available, like benches, patio furniture, or outdoor barstools.

KEEP/TOSS CLUE: For the enjoyment of those seated behind you, many outdoor venues have put restrictions in place regarding the style and size of the chair you are allowed to bring. Check with your venue, but the average back height permitted seems to be 40".

KEEP

No more than three outdoor blankets that:

- are compact and easy to fold

- are large enough to be useful

- are thick enough to provide comfort

TOSS

Blankets that:

- are not machine-washable or easily cleaned

- are too full of holes or too worn to sit on comfortably

Did you know?

You can turn any blanket into a water-resistant one by laying a plastic tablecloth underneath your blanket (plastic side down) to keep the blanket dry on damp ground.

KEEP

One hard-sided cooler that:

- is durable and sturdy

- works well to keep your items cool

- has wide wheels for easy maneuvering

- has a drain plug for easy cleaning

- has a stain- and odor-resistant liner

- has a 12-plus drink can capacity

- fits 2-liter bottles upright

TOSS

Hard-sided coolers that:

- don't keep perishable foods cool enough to be safe (below 40° F)

- are difficult to pack and unpack

- have a lingering odor that cannot be cleaned

- have a broken closure latch

- have difficult-to-use handles that make carrying the cooler challenging

- are awkward to maneuver

KEEP
One soft-sided cooler that:

- has a padded shoulder strap for comfy carrying

- has a convenient front slip pocket for extra storage

- is in good condition

- has ample room for multiple cold packs

TOSS
Soft-sided coolers that:

- have a broken zipper

- are torn or smell bad

- don't keep food cold enough to be safe

- aren't the correct size to carry what you need

- are awkward or difficult to carry

Did you know?

These are the most common cooler sizes, along with the approximate number of 12-oz. drink cans each holds:

9 quarts = 13 cans

24 quarts = 24 cans

50 quarts = 72 cans

110 quarts = 150 cans

14 Items to Keep in a Fun-in-the-Sun Bag

1. After-sun lotion
2. Antibacterial wipes
3. Beach or picnic blanket
4. Dry paintbrush for dusting sand off feet
5. Frisbee
6. Flip-flops
7. Hair ties
8. Insect repellent
9. Lip balm with SPF
10. Sand toys
11. Sun visor or hat
12. Sunblock
13. Sunglasses
14. Swimsuit cover-up

KEEP
These sand and water toys:

- fins that are in good repair without any cracks or breaks
- snorkel that can be cleaned and has been recently washed
- face mask that doesn't leak
- goggles that aren't too tight or too loose
- water sprinkler that sprays a gentle stream for kids to run through
- inflatable rafts in good condition
- water guns that shoot a good stream of water

TOSS
These sand and water toys:

- broken goggles
- popped or torn inflatable toys
- faded and gross beach balls
- outgrown water wings
- anything plastic that is now brittle from age or being stored in hot temperatures
- water guns that are broken, dangerous, difficult to use, or don't hold water

Chapter 11
Crafting and Hobbies

Now is the time to address all the leftovers from the many interests, hobbies, phases, and pastimes you've had through the years. It's also time to admit you're not going to refinish that dresser, build that doghouse, or string that necklace. Once you do that, the more time, space, and energy you'll have to devote to the hobbies that currently interest you!

The key to organizing your crafting and hobby supplies is to give yourself a specific amount of storage space per current interest or hobby and then to organize into that space. In this chapter, I will show you what to keep and what to toss for the most common hobbies. If you are a serial hobbyist, then most sections will apply. And if a specific hobby of yours is not mentioned by name, you can still look over the lists to get a general idea of the quantity and condition of things you will want to keep or toss.

Just so we are clear, you are under no obligation to keep anything you make. I repeat: You have permission to toss items you hand made. Many times, the most enjoyable part is creating the item, not keeping it around to clutter your home.

Ask yourself these key questions:
1. Does this have all the pieces and directions?
2. Am I holding on to this because I think I should love it or because I spent some time working on it?
3. Am I ever really going to finish this project?

Let's toss the stuff you don't use so that when you have the time to craft, you can actually get to the fun part instead of wasting time sorting through supplies.

Crafting Supplies

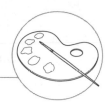

KEEP

These beading/jewelry-making items:

- chain-wire cutters that are still sharp enough to get the job done

- bead and thread cord that is the right size to fit the beads you work with

- 3 pairs of pliers: round-nose, flat-nose, and crimp pliers

- 12 spools in a combination of beading cord, thread, and memory wire

- clasps, headpins, and eye pins

- crimp and other beads

- tape measure with easy-to-read measurements

- adhesive that works for plastic, wood, and metal

TOSS

These beading/jewelry-making items:

- spools of wire and thread that don't have enough left to complete a project

- tape measure that is difficult to read or work with, risking an inaccurate measurement

- adhesives that have dried up

- beads or embellishments you know you will never use

- beads, wires, or supplies for projects you don't do, like earring wires if you never make earrings

KEEP/TOSS CLUE: Keeping too much of a specific supply of items, like beads, means you won't be able to find what you are looking for when you need it. Designate a specific container for beads, and when it is full, use (or toss) what you have before you get more. This prevents the collection from getting out of control.

KEEP

**These items for drawing/painting/
sketching:**

- paintbrushes that are clean and do not have a tendency to shed bristles

- sketch pads that open easily and are comfortable to work in

- watercolors and oil paints you still use

- an easel that fits your usual conditions (such as a tabletop model versus a standing model)

- a palette that is easy to hold and to clean

- a good pencil sharpener (if you use drawing pencils)

TOSS

**These items for drawing/painting/
sketching:**

- dried-up markers

- markers with mushy tips

- doubles and triples of the same marker, pencil, or paint color

- paints that have dried out

- broken pencils and pastels

- calligraphy set that has never come out of the plastic wrap

- dried-up ink cartridges or bottles

- paintbrushes that shed bristles

- paintbrushes with stuck-together bristles

- bottles with so little in them that they are not worth saving

---

STORAGE SOLUTION

Take a photo of an open box of supplies or an open drawer of supplies. Then tape the photo to the box or drawer front. That way, it'll only take a glance for you to know what is stored where. Bonus points if you keep the same photo on your smartphone so you have the picture with you at the store when you are tempted to buy more, and you can see what, if anything, you are missing.

KEEP

These items for knitting or crocheting:

- 3 sets of your favorite crochet hooks and/or knitting needles

- 1 yarn or tapestry needle

- yarn and patterns that you plan to use within a year

- up to 3 reliable stitch holders

- sharp scissors for cutting fibers easily and cleanly

TOSS

These items for knitting or crocheting:

- any supplies or patterns that are too novice or expert for your level

- plastic needles that snag yarn or aluminum needles that yarn easily slips off of

- needles that are too fancy to work with, like ones with light-up tips

- yarn in the wrong weight or color for the projects you prefer to take on

- yarn that is difficult to work with, like lace weight

- supplies that were purchased on sale with no pattern in mind

> **STORAGE SOLUTION**
>
> Designate a 1-gallon zip-top bag as the place to store all those might-need-it-one-day, almost-all-used-up balls of yarn. While 12 inches of red yarn won't make a sweater, it could be the perfect mouth for a teddy bear.

KEEP

These model-building tools:

- still-sharp hobby knife

- sandpaper with the right grit as to not damage projects

TOSS

These model-building tools:

- dried-out bottles of glue

- sandpaper that has little to no grit left on it

KEEP

These scrapbooking/card-making supplies:

- 1 pad of solid paper and 1 pad of patterned paper (about 180 sheets each, in the size for the albums you create)

- refillable tape runner with extra refills

- five basic paper punches that punch cleanly

- pens that write easily and do not smear

- scrapbooking albums

- rub-ons in themes you work with

- stickers and chipboard punch-outs in colors or themes you like

- borders, die cuts, rhinestones, buttons, and blossoms that are in good condition and work for your projects

TOSS

These scrapbooking/card-making supplies:

- empty tape runners that cannot be refilled

- stickers and adhesive embellishments that no longer stick

- rubber stamps you don't use

- albums in sizes you don't work with

- albums that are not photo-safe (acid-free)

- page protectors that do not fit the album size you use

- excess quantities of paper

- rub-ons with parts of the design missing

- pens or markers that are dried out, do not show on the paper, or have a pointed tip that rips the paper

- chipboard accents that are so thick they make the pages too bulky

- borders, tags, flowers, buttons, brads, and eyelets that do not work with the style of albums or cards you create (like antique designs if you prefer contemporary)

- organizers with nothing in them because they are not the right size or are not easy to use

Here's a rough guide to what you need to create (12) 12" x 12" embellished album pages:

- (12) 12" x 12" solid/ patterned scrapbook papers
- 24 stickers
- 48 embellishments (like rhinestones, buttons, or tags)
- 96 chipboard pieces

KEEP
These sewing and quilting items:

- sharp fabric scissors (one large pair and one small)
- material in the colors and weights you tend to use frequently
- spools of embroidery thread with enough left on them to work with
- fabric-marking pencils (one for light and one for dark fabrics)
- an easy-to-read ruler or tape measure
- rotary cutter
- 100 straight pins

TOSS
These sewing and quilting items:

- duplicates and triplicates of the same sewing needles
- seam rippers that aren't sharp enough to work well
- excessive spools of thread (40 in varying colors should be enough to give you a wide variety to match any project)
- thread that jams your sewing machine or breaks easily
- scraps of material that have little or no value
- fabric scissors that are not sharp and pull the fabric or have gotten sticky and can't be cleaned
- replacement blades for a rotary cutter you no longer own

KEEP

These pottery and clay items:

- clay that is still useful

- brushes and sponges that are clean enough to reuse

- paint that doesn't clump, in colors you like

TOSS

These pottery and clay items:

- jars of glaze with too little left to finish a project

- dried-up clays and paints

- old brushes

KEEP

These woodworking and refinishing tools:

- claw hammer

- chisel that is easy to grip and works well

- sharp utility knife in good condition

- easy-to-read tape measure

- painter's tape that leaves a clean line

- sandpaper in a variety of grits

- work gloves that fit and are easy to maneuver when wearing them

- stains in colors you like and that generally work with your projects

KEEP/TOSS CLUE: You usually buy fasteners for a project when you pick out the other pieces. So unless you constantly build the same type of thing over and over, like a birdhouse, and always need the same size fasteners in multiples, follow the rule of 500. Keep 500 (or fewer) fasteners spread between the following categories, which comes to about 50 of each:

- tiny nails (½")
- small nails (1")
- medium nails (2")
- large nails (3")
- extra-large nails (4")
- small screws (1")
- medium screws (3")
- large screws (6")
- tacks (1")
- brads (1")

TOSS

These woodworking tools:

- wood glue, putties, and fillers that have dried up

- excessive quantities of fasteners (nails, brads, screws, and tacks)

- a level that is not giving you an accurate reading

- lumber scraps for the birdhouse or dollhouse you never built

- pieces you planned to refinish but have not

- pieces you have no place to store

- rusty cans of stains and finishes

- stains that do not apply as promised

- sealers that leave a cloudy residue on your finished project

- project-specific stains you'll likely never use again

- topcoats that never dry correctly or remain tacky too long

Did you know?

You can donate building supplies, like coffee cans filled with nails or other excess supplies, to Habitat for Humanity Restores. Check them out at habitat.org/restores.

KEEP

These photography accessories:

- cameras you still use and that work properly

- tripod that fits your current cameras

- filters for cameras you currently own

- extra batteries for cameras you own

TOSS

These photography accessories:

- lens-cleaning cloths that do not clean well

- camera bag with missing strap or that doesn't fit your camera

- cords and accessories for cameras you no longer own

KEEP
These items for making soap/candles/candy:

- accurate scale in gram weights

- 10-quart pot that heats evenly

- measuring spoons that still have legible measurements

- candy melts and fondants that are 18 months old or newer

TOSS
These items for making soap/candles/candy:

- molds or pans that are warped, dented, or have coating that is flaking

- molds or pans whose designs you no longer like

- candy melts that melt unevenly when you test, are oily, or seize (all are a sign of them being past their prime)

- candy melts that taste chalky or dusty

- food coloring that has dried up

- any bottle that makes it difficult to dispense the product in the proper quantities

- dull knives that don't leave a smooth edge

- essential oils that are three years or older and may have degraded properties, especially if they've been stored in sunlight or warm temperatures

KEEP

Floral-arranging items such as:

- stem and florist's tape that unrolls easily

- sand, shells, glass marbles, and other vase accessories you still like

- artificial floral items that are in good condition, like silk flowers or greenery

- moss that is in good condition

- cutting pliers that are sharp enough to do the job and comfortable enough to hold

- wreath form and other containers

TOSS

Floral-arranging items such as:

- silk flowers or greenery that is faded, fraying, torn, or dusty beyond cleaning

- flowers with obviously missing petals or leaves

- ribbon that is discolored or unraveling

- spools of ribbon that have too little to wrap a bow around even a small vase

- broken or crumbling floral foam bricks

- moss that is crumbling or falling apart

- dull shears

- excessive numbers of flower vases

Chapter 12
Sports and Activities

You can be game-time ready all the time by keeping the equipment for the sports and activities you currently engage in sorted and organized. Who needs more dust-gatherers lying around? Not you. A good rule of thumb is the one-year rule: If you have played the sport or enjoyed the activity more than once in the past year, then keep the equipment; if not, toss it!

Also toss broken or otherwise compromised equipment that can cause injury. This includes outgrown equipment; most items have recommended age, weight, and height guidelines.

High-priced items, such as exercise equipment, can be difficult to part with, but you can feel good about donating it to people who will really use it—and reclaiming the space for you to enjoy the activities you actually do regularly.

Ask yourself these key questions:

1. Am I still involved in this activity?
2. Could I easily borrow or rent this equipment when I want to use it?
3. If I were moving, would I pay to have it packed and shipped?

Ready, set, toss!

Ball-Centered Sports and Games

KEEP

Helmets that:

- you still like

- can be adjusted for a snug fit

- include a safety approval sticker (CPSC, ASTM, or Snell)

- have working chinstraps that keep them in place

TOSS

Helmets that:

- have been in a crash

- were dropped so hard the foam cracked

- are from 1970 or before, as these no longer meet current safety requirements

- are constructed of foam only

- are bent or severely dented

- have a facemask that isn't fully intact

- have rusted bolts

- are five-plus years old (when most manufacturers suggest a replacement, because materials degrade with use, and when stored in warm conditions)

Did you know?

Most sports and activities require a helmet. Others may be safer with one even if not required, so you might consider investing in one anyway, no matter what your age.

KEEP

Balls that:

- are regulation size and weight

- are correct for your course or playing surface, like turf or grass

- have good air retention or bounce, if applicable

- still have a good grip or proper traction

- are built for a high launch and long flight (golf) or are otherwise designed to maximize your game

TOSS

Balls that:

- don't stay inflated

- are peeling, cracked, scratched, no longer true to their original shape, or otherwise compromised

- have loose or pulled-apart stitches

- are too worn to be useful

- don't offer a good rebound

- are too slick or slippery

- give undesirable spin

- are easily damaged

- are the wrong type of balls for your course or playing surface

KEEP/TOSS CLUE: Some sporting centers, like those with indoor basketball courts, prefer you use separate balls for indoor play and outdoor play so as not to scratch and wear out nicely polished indoor surfaces. If you regularly play in both indoor and outdoor conditions, keep one ball for each. If you only play in one or the other, or your local activity center doesn't make a distinction with your usage, just keep one ball for each sport.

STORAGE SOLUTION

Round up sports balls and store them in a mesh laundry bag that can be hung from a hook. Since the bag is breathable, balls can be stored damp without fear of growing mildewy.

KEEP

Golf clubs that:

- make a complete set

- are of a good weight for your game

- are designed for your current skill level (not too novice or advanced)

- have an intact grip without any tears

TOSS

Golf clubs that are:

- bent or dented

- rusted

- too tall or too short for your golf swing

- too heavy or too light

- unnecessary extras

KEEP

Golf tees that:

- are in good condition

- hold the ball well

TOSS

Golf tees that:

- are malformed or otherwise don't hold the ball steady

- you have too many of, like mulitple boxes of the same tee

- are the wrong type for your playing course

- are splintering, crooked, or otherwise damaged

---

6 Coaching Must-Haves

If you regularly coach sports or other activities, you'll want to keep your:

1. Ball inflator/pump, if needed
2. Clipboard
3. Field markers and cones
4. Megaphone
5. Stopwatch
6. Whistle

KEEP

Hockey and lacrosse sticks that:

- have the correct alignment for your hand preference
- have a good grip
- are the correct size

TOSS

Hockey and lacrosse sticks that have:

- worn blades
- cheap blades
- cheap construction
- cracks or splinters
- a tendency to bend too much, especially once it heats up during play
- frayed or worn netting (lacrosse)

KEEP

Hockey gloves that have:

- a good palm grip
- vents for breathability
- easy-flex thumbs
- the correct sizing for your hands
- durable construction

TOSS

Hockey gloves that are:

- too thin to offer suitable protection
- too snug
- difficult to take on and off
- torn or overly worn in the lining or exterior
- nonadjustable
- a nontapered fit, so they tend to slide off

STORAGE SOLUTION

A tall, outdoor trash can is an easy way to store sticks and bats.

KEEP

Soccer shin guards that are:

- the correct size

- molded to conform to your shin

- breathable

- comfortable protection

- good with moisture control

- backed with bonded foam for cushioning

- washable

Did you know?

There are five standard sizes of soccer balls:

- 1 and 2: promotional sizes
- 3: ages 8 and younger
- 4: ages 8 to 12
- 5: ages 12 and older

TOSS

Soccer shin guards that:

- have broken straps

- dig into legs

- fall down or slip during play

- are built into sock and not repositional

- are too tall (interferes with running)

- always move out of place

STORAGE SOLUTION

If you are a coach, team uniforms and paperwork can overrun your home and car. Keep a portable file box in your car with all the required paperwork and plenty of pens for parents to fill out forms as needed.

KEEP
Football shoulder/arm pads and padded pants that:

- are the right size for the player

- have easy-on arm or leg openings

- hold up well through play and washings

TOSS
Football shoulder/arm pads and padded pants that:

- have been damaged and no longer offer proper protection

- chafe the skin

- don't remain firmly in place during play

KEEP
One mouth guard that is:

- comfortable

- compatible with braces (if needed)

TOSS
Mouth guards that:

- are stretched out of shape

- taste bad

- never molded properly to the wearer's mouth

- are cracked or broken

- irritate the wearer's mouth when worn

- make the wearer's lips stick out, risking further injury

KEEP/TOSS CLUE: Many sports and activities require special footwear. Toss the obvious—the outgrown cleats or the ones for sports that are no longer played. Also look for shoes that are worn down, have diminished support, have tears in the material, are separating from the sole, or have lacing holes that are no longer tight enough.

KEEP

Softball/baseball bats that:

- are the proper length and weight for their use

- are a solid construction but not dangerous

- have a barrel size that is not too thin or too thick

- are right for the type of ball, the venue, and the age of the players

TOSS

Bats that have:

- a slippery grip

- a crack, split, or chip

- a loose knob

- too narrow a diameter for an "amateur" player to hit with

KEEP

Tennis racquets that:

- are strung tightly for good play

- have a good grip and enough room for your hand

- are not too heavy or too light

TOSS

Tennis racquets that:

- are cheaply made

- are warped

- have a slippery grip

- are too short in the grip for your hands

KEEP/TOSS CLUE: Keep gloves with an adjustable strap for a good fit. Toss those that are worn out or need a repair you can't make or won't pay to have done.

Billiards

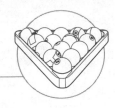

KEEP

These billiard supplies:

- 15 pool balls (numbered 1–15), plus one cue ball that rolls straight

- ball rack that fits all the balls for setting up the game

- table brush in good condition, with bristles that do the job

- cue chalk that has a good texture and applies evenly

TOSS

These billiard supplies:

- cracked balls

- splintering wooden ball racks

- cracked plastic ball racks

- cue chalk that is crumbling, doesn't match your table surface so as to hide marks, is too dusty, or is mostly used up

KEEP

Billiard cues that:

- are of sufficient weight

- are regulation length and shape

- have joints that tighten and stay tight

- suit your skill level

TOSS

Billiard cues that:

- are bent or warped or have a crooked, scratched, or dented tip or stick

- are improperly tipped or missing their tips altogether

- have a fraying or tearing wrap on the grip surface

- have loose weight bolts

- have joints that operate incorrectly

- have a chipped or flaking clear coat

- are the wrong size, weight, or are otherwise uncomfortable to use

Bowling

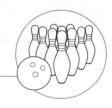

KEEP
One bowling ball per player that is:

- in good condition

- the correct bowling weight for you

- comfortable for your finger span

- comfortable to play with

- a color or style that you still like

TOSS
Bowling balls that:

- have finger holes that are too tight or too loose

- won't hook (meant for straight shots only)

- are cracked or chipped

- are too heavy or too light, based on your skill level

Did you know?

You can give bowling balls that are just a little scuffed and scratched new life with a professional polish. And you can give your unwanted balls to a local bowling alley for new generations to enjoy.

Yoga/Exercising/Weight Lifting

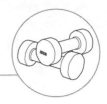

KEEP
These exercise machines:

- an exercise bike you use
- an elliptical machine that works
- an all-around workout machine that's easy to use
- anything that works the muscle groups you want to target

TOSS
Exercise machines that:

- have turned into makeshift clothes closets
- are older versions of upgraded models
- have broken belts or no longer work
- are squeaky and can't be oiled or are otherwise too loud to operate
- have nonfunctioning electronic components
- you just don't use

KEEP
These workout accessories, if you use them at home:

- bands that offer the resistance you need
- straps if they close securely
- mats with the correct amount of give and cushion for your activity

TOSS
Workout accessories that you don't use, such as:

- jump ropes
- exercise balls
- steps, especially if they are unstable
- blocks, especially if they have pieces missing

KEEP

These workout-enhancing weights:

- weighted vest that still fits

- arm weights that strap on well and are comfortable

- dumbells or kettle bells you actually use

Did you know?

Worn-out yoga mats make great pads for kneeling in the garden.

TOSS

Weights that:

- won't stay on or are uncomfortable to use

- are too light to be useful

- are too heavy and therefore dangerous

- you no longer use for whatever reason

KEEP/TOSS CLUE: If you don't know what a given workout accessory or exercise machine is or how it works, toss it!

STORAGE SOLUTION
....

Hang a stuffed animal hammock in the corner of a room or garage to stash that oversize, inflated exercise ball.

Walking/Running

KEEP

Wearable fitness trackers/pedometers that:

- sync with other technology, such as a smartphone

- are accurate

- keep cumulative totals

- have an easy-to-read display

- track steps, calories, and distance

- are sensitive enough to record activity

- include a heart-rate monitor

- are waterproof

- have a replaceable band

- are "easy on"

TOSS

Wearable fitness trackers/pedometers that:

- are too easy to accidentally reset

- won't set to customize to your stride

- are so sensitive they give inaccurate readings

- are difficult to program

- are uncomfortable to wear

- have a short battery life

- slip off clothing (so they're easy to lose)

KEEP

Sneakers that are:

- a good fit

- appropriate for your activity

- cushioned

- arch-supported

TOSS

Sneakers that:

- rub painfully on your foot

- are worn in the tread

- are too worn to be supportive

Did you know?

It is recommended to replace old, worn-out shoes at the 300-mile mark to prevent injury due to loss of shock absorption and stability. Worn-out sneakers can be ground down to make new play surfaces, like playgrounds, with Nike's reuse-a-shoe program (learn more at Nike.com), and you can give any still-good sneakers you just don't wear or like to Soles4souls.org.

Gymnastics/Dance

KEEP

This gymnastics/dance equipment:

- 3 hair nets

- 5 hair ties that match the wearer's hair color

- 1 box of bobby pins

- nude or flesh-tone undergarments

- bra with clear straps (if needed)

- glitter spray or roll-on body glitter

- nail polish remover

- leotards that still fit, are the correct style and color for your activity, and are washable and easy to care for

TOSS

This gymnastics/dance equipment:

- tights with runs in them

- bottles of glitter spray that are used up or dried out

- fashion tape that is not sticky

- equipment bags that are ripping or have broken straps

STORAGE SOLUTION

Zip-top bags are the best way to keep costume-specific items together, like gloves and hairpieces. Write the list directly on the bag so you have a checklist to ensure you have everything you need.

STORAGE SOLUTION

Keep costumes organized and wrinkle-free by keeping them in a garment bag.

Music

KEEP

These musical instruments and accessories:

- instruments currently played by members of the household

- sheet music to go with any of the instruments

- extra pieces and replacement parts for the currently used instruments

TOSS

Musical instruments and accessories that:

- are damaged beyond repair

- no one in the house plays

Fishing

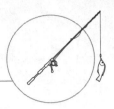

KEEP
Fishing poles that are:

- the right size, weight, and style for the type of fishing you do, like saltwater or ice

- in good working order and not damaged or cracked

- have all their parts, like reels and grips

- intact at the rod tips

TOSS
Fishing poles that are:

- rusted, broken, or bent

- not meant for the type of fishing you do

- made of cheap materials that won't hold up

- no longer casting easily

KEEP
Tackle box and tackle-box gear that:

- is large enough to accommodate all your supplies

- has a locking lid to prevent spillage

- is suitable for the type of fishing you usually do

- is in good condition or can be easily repaired (and you will take the time to repair it)

TOSS
This tackle box and tackle-box gear:

- gear that is rusty, bent, or broken

- gear of an excessive amount you could never use up, like six boxes of similar lures

- lures, hooks, or floats for kinds of fishing you no longer do

- spools of line that are hopelessly knotted

- spools of line with too little left on them to be useful

- floats, hooks, or flies that are no longer in good condition

Outdoor Games and Lawn Activities

KEEP

Outdoor game accessories and supplies that:

- have carrying cases in good condition

- have a working zipper

- are easy to assemble and disassemble

- stay together while playing

- have all the necessary parts to play the game

- are safe for children (if children are playing)

- are durable enough to withstand rough outdoor play

- are portable enough to take to tailgates, the beach, or BBQs

TOSS

Outdoor game accessories and supplies that:

- are made of particle board that is warping or coming apart at the edges

- are the "kid" versions of adult games when you need the adult versions

- have a lacquer finish or paint that is peeling

- are broken and unable to be fixed or not worth the effort

- do not work as they are supposed to

- are not fun to play

- no one knows how to play

KEEP
Supplies for ball-centered lawn games you play regularly, such as:

- the newest version of a ladder ball

- bolas (projectiles you throw at targets) that are not easily tangled

- a complete croquet set with 6 wood mallets and 6 balls

- 8 bocce balls and 1 pallino ball

- equipment that is heavy enough to play with on a windy day

- lawn bowling pins with wide and heavy bases to stand on grass

TOSS
These supplies for ball-centered lawn games:

- equipment with ropes that tangle

- equipment with joints on ladders that fall apart

- water-filled balls that can leak

- equipment with wood handles that are splintering

- croquet mallets with missing caps on the heads

- bocce set with missing pallino ball

KEEP
These tossing-game supplies:

- bean bags that are weighty enough to toss

- safer versions of originals, like rubber horseshoes versus metal

- lawn darts with plastic tips

- ring toss set with all the rings accounted for

TOSS
These tossing-game supplies:

- lawn darts with steel tips, which can hurt someone

- broken cast horseshoes

- bean bags that are torn or ripping

- flimsy stakes that bend under the weight of horseshoes hitting them

- anything that damages your lawn or causes deep divots

KEEP

Kites, flying disks, and boomerangs that are:

- durable

- fun to play with

- actually flyable

- in a bright, visible color

- comfortable to throw

- easy to catch

- easy to fold and unfold (kites)

TOSS

Kites, flying disks, and boomerangs that:

- are damaged

- have strings that are hopelessly tangled (spools of kite line)

- are flimsy or too thin to take flight and stay afloat

- have gouged, cracked, or split plastic

- are lopsided and unable to fly well

- don't float well, making for a frustrating game

- float way too long, so you risk losing them over a fence

- light up (like flying disks) but are so bright that they are difficult to look at in the dark, or they need expensive or not-readily-available batteries

Biking

KEEP
These bikes and biking supplies:

- bikes that are easy and comfortable to ride

- bikes built for the terrain you typically ride on

- padded biking shorts

- bikes with all parts in good working order

- tires that inflate and stay inflated

TOSS
These bikes and biking supplies:

- bikes with pedals that cause your feet to slip

- bikes with brakes that do not work and can't be fixed

- bikes with uncomfortable seats that aren't adjustable or replaceable

- bikes that have rusted parts

- bikes with weakened welds (which happens over time)

- tires that are rotted or leaking beyond repair

- chains that are broken and can't easily be put back on or repaired

- bike rack for a car that either does not fit your current bike or is missing pieces

- bike rack that bikes do not fit securely into

- bike rack for your car that damages or scratches your car

- torn cycling gloves or gloves missing a mate

- cracked or old water bottles

- bike locks that are missing the key or have an unknown combination

- broken or cracked bike lights

Surf/Body/Paddleboarding

KEEP
Surf/body/paddleboards that:

- have an attached leash for safety

- are bright, visible colors with designs you like

- have a length or width that is still suitable for your body

- work for the style of boarding you like to do

TOSS
Surf/body/paddleboard equipment that is:

- simply worn out

- dented or dinged

- missing the fin

- caked or crumbling and no longer useful (tubs of board wax)

KEEP
Personal floatation devices (lifejackets) that:

- are United States Coast Guard (USCG) certified

- have a quick-release buckle

- are the proper size and within the weight restrictions for the people who will use them

- are vented to keep you cooler

- have tabs or pockets for keeping small items on hand, like an ID or a whistle

TOSS
Personal floatation devices (lifejackets) that:

- chafe your skin

- do not allow you to move freely

- have a faded color or are lacking reflective tape, so they are less visible

Skiing/Snowboarding

KEEP
This skiing/snowboarding equipment:

- skis or snowboards that fit and are in good repair

- poles with functioning straps and that are the right height for your torso

- boots that are the proper level for your skiing ability and have solid bindings

- ski suits that fit and have working zippers

- skis or snowboards with adjustable mounting holes for boots

TOSS
This skiing/snowboarding equipment:

- helmets that have taken hard hits

- helmets that do not fit properly or that do not have a working strap

- skis or snowboards that are not resort-approved, like those without a steel edge

- broken or chipped snowboards

- snowboards with dull edges

- boots or clothing that are uncomfortable

KEEP
Ski goggles that:

- are antifreezing

- are vented

- are fog resistant

- have an adjustable fit

TOSS
Ski goggles that:

- don't easily fit over your helmet, making them difficult to put on and easy to lose

- have scratched lenses

- have lenses that are too dark or too light, making it difficult to see

Hiking/Camping

KEEP

Backpacks that are:

- in good repair, with working zippers and flaps

- the right size for your needs; not too large or too small

TOSS

Backpacks that are:

- too heavy to carry comfortably when full

- worn, fraying, or unable to be cleaned

- moldy or mildewed

KEEP

Sleeping bags that:

- are "mummy" style or have a hood, if you need it for temperature control

- are quick-drying inside and out

- have a pocket for a makeshift pillow

- have an R value for the conditions in which you most often camp

TOSS

Sleeping bags that:

- have broken zippers, are torn, or have fraying material

- are itchy, scratchy, too small, or otherwise uncomfortable to sleep in

- are moldy or mildewed

- aren't suitable for the conditions in which you most often camp

- can't be compressed (if you backpack all your gear in and out of campsites)

Chapter 13
Keepsakes and Photographs

Are your precious family keepsakes and treasured photographs sitting in boxes, rarely seen or used? We've all been there, digging through boxes of family treasures, wondering if we should keep a favorite book, first teddy bear, or Grandma's candlesticks to be used and cherished by future generations. After all, part of the joy in passing items down is that it makes us feel we'll be connected to future generations.

But if you have things boxed up, they may be at risk of being damaged while in storage. And when you save it all, the good stuff gets lost in the mess. Armed with the knowledge of knowing just the right items to save will help you the next time you ask yourself, "Should I keep this for my daughter or grandson?"

Then there are the photographs, ah… the photographs. Duplicates of a blurry landscape somewhere in the world, negatives that are too brittle to be viewed, and a black-and-white photo portrait of a woman in a hat, with no name written on the back. Given some time and clear sorting guidelines, you can pare down the porcelain figurines and photographs to just the ones it makes sense to keep.

Ask yourself these key questions:
1. Am I holding on to this out of obligation, expectation, or guilt?
2. Do I have anything else that reminds me of this good time or lost loves?
3. If I took a picture of it, would that make it easier for me to let it go?

Now let's get started so you can get a clearer picture of your future without all the stuff.

Print Photographs

KEEP

Photographs that are:

- flattering to all those in the picture

- from events you want to remember

- of people you know or can identify (unless it is an old photo and the connection may be found through a genealogical search)

- capturing a person's personality, even if you know it might not be that person's favorite shot (if you love it, keep it)

- nice photos of you (even if you don't love how you look, other people will, and by tossing them all, you risk deleting yourself from family history)

- perhaps not technically great but that really capture the emotion and feeling of a moment

TOSS

Photographs that are:

- of unknown subjects, such as photos mistakenly taken of the floor or ceiling

- blurry or otherwise out of focus

- too similar, like multiples of the same group of people, pets, or landscapes, just in slightly different poses/angles

- of random landscapes no one can identify

- stuck together and cannot be pried apart

- moldy, faded, torn, or brittle

- of people or events you don't remember or would prefer not to be reminded of

KEEP

Photo boxes that:

- have tabbed index cards to help you label and categorize what's inside

- are of sturdy, acid-free cardboard construction with reinforced corners or archival-quality plastic cases

- have a standard metal holder on the outside for a label

- coordinate with your decor, if you choose to display the box on your bookcase or other open spaces

- are a size suitable for your storage needs (if you have lots of large school portraits, you need larger, shallower boxes than if you have mostly 3" x 5" or 4" x 6" prints)

TOSS

Photo boxes that:

- are not acid-free and therefore not safe for long-term storage

- lack corresponding lids, leaving the photos open to air and light

- feature snap-together sides that can come undone under the weight of the photographs

---

Did you know?

Turn the chore of photo sorting into a memory-making moment. Invite extended family members over, bring out the photos, and share stories. Some people may love to take back old photos or postcards they sent you while traveling. If you want, you can scan the old photos and make a photo book using Chatbook, Shutterfly, or other similar services.

KEEP THIS, TOSS THAT

Memorabilia

KEEP
Three treasured toys that:

- were your favorites

- were hot trends, like Cabbage Patch Kids, Lalaloopsy dolls, or others

- store well

- you have the storage space for

- are unique, uncommon, or handmade

TOSS
Toys that:

- may have been recalled

- are a possible safety concern

- won't clean up well after being in storage, like ones that have plastic faces that can yellow over time

KEEP/TOSS CLUE: We often hold on to childhood toys, believing future grandchildren will love to play with them, but sadly this is not often the case. Toys rarely survive storage intact. If the toy does make it, many times pieces have gone missing. Then there are concerns over safety standards. Choking hazards, lead paint, sharp corners, and recalled items are only a few of the many possible dangers of old toys. Not to mention he or she may simply not be as enamored with the toy as you were.

KEEP

These pieces of mundane memorabilia:

- an item from your first or favorite job, like your business card

- something of significance that you carry every day in your purse, like your makeup bag

- a treasure related to your favorite hobby, like a handmade pincushion for your sewing projects

- a piece or a few pieces representing your favorite spots in the world, like shells from the beach or a bottle of wine from your trip to Napa Valley

- a memento from a childhood haunt, like a postcard or your mess kit from summer camp

- a representation of a skill or talent, like a vest you crocheted or a poem you wrote

TOSS

Mundane memorabilia that:

- will not keep well in storage

- are multiple representations of the same event, time, or place

- are too large to store

- are not that meaningful—your first briefcase: possibly; your third: not so much

KEEP/TOSS CLUE: We love discovering little-known facts about our loved ones. At first glance, a set of blueprints and a compass might look like junk. That is, until you hear the story of how Grandpa was a total architectural buff who could name the designers of all the great buildings and whose lifelong dream was designing the world's tallest skyscraper. Learning the meaning behind the memorabilia makes all the difference. Framing such a blueprint to hang on your office wall would make it decorative, but more importantly, you would have a daily reminder of Grandpa.

Children's Keepsakes

Between noodle-encrusted, glitter-covered artwork and every greeting card you ever received, it can be difficult to let some of your child's treasures go. You probably have important items and keepsakes stashed in shopping bags and tucked in drawers around your house. Go through every room and gather all of your children's keepsakes so you can review them with the following guidelines in mind.

KEEP

One of each of these items from your child's most precious years:

Infancy

- blanket
- onesie
- first holiday bib
- ceremonial clothing
- favorite outfit
- first stuffed toy
- baby bottle
- outfit from hospital
- sunhat
- tiny unused diaper

Toddlerhood

- pair of tiny shoes
- piece of artwork per month
- sweater
- toy
- first tie or dress
- engraved item
- favorite book
- favorite hat
- favorite stuffed toy
- lock of hair
- recipes of favorite dishes

- trophies, ribbons, medals, and certificates, like preschool graduation

Childhood
- special artwork piece per month

- report cards and progress reports

- certificates noting special accomplishments, like Second Grader of the Month

- medals

- postcards from family trips

- printed-out e-mails and texts

- programs from plays and recitals

- recipes of the food they made for the first time

Did you know?

Trophy makers can remove the engraved plaque for you to keep and you can donate the rest of the trophy. Or take a photo and donate the entire trophy to be re-engraved and used again.

KEEP/TOSS CLUE: Just because your child created it does not mean you are obligated to keep it. The painted plate from art class, the paper-bag puppet from scouting, and the hand-sewn pillow are precious, but they are not all keepers. In storage, the pillow will become musty with age, and anyone can glue googly eyes to a brown bag; therefore, the plate is the keeper!

STORAGE SOLUTION

Unused pizza boxes can be the perfect storage option for artwork created by your child. The rule: one box per child per year.

KEEP
The following items, if you have a pet:

- "baby" teeth
- tags
- first collar
- favorite blanket
- favorite or first toy
- food dish
- fur clipping
- paw imprint or mold

TOSS
Pet toys, blankets, or other items that:

- don't have any special memories attached to them
- are smelly, moldy, or dirty

KEEP
Holiday decorations that:

- have special meaning
- you can use year after year

TOSS
Holiday decorations that are:

- possible hazards, like ones that have frayed wires or broken glass
- too degraded, worn, or faded to be used
- something you dislike so much you never, ever bring them out

KEEP/TOSS CLUE: In moderation, holiday decorations are one of the easiest treasures to save and share, since they are stored away for most of the year. So many of us have traditions that revolve around holidays, which is another reason decorations are special to us. Without the story behind it, the dish the green-bean casserole is traditionally served in is just a dish. Capture the story behind an item to turn it into something more meaningful. Know who gave it to your grandmother and when it was purchased? Write this information on a piece of paper and store it with the item.

Memento Clothing

KEEP

This everyday clothing:

- an entire ensemble, complete with belt and accessories

- one item you wore all the time

- your favorite pair of jeans and a well-loved T-shirt

TOSS

This everyday clothing:

- any item that was so trendy that you barely wore it yourself—if you're going to keep something, make it something you actually wore for more than a season

- anything made of wool or silk, since these degrade in storage and can attract bugs

---

3 Best Keepsake Keeps

1. Your single most loved item. The book you read over and over as a teenager, the CD you played again and again. A favorite pair of pants washed and worn a thousand times, or the teddy bear you carried everywhere as a child.

2. Physical representations of a positive experience, like the first set of dishes you bought with your own money when you moved out on your own or the poster you bought when you toured Europe before college.

3. Your favorite representation of a significant life event. You could keep one of many items from a 50th birthday party, such as a cocktail napkin, a party favor, or a birthday hat. Which one is your favorite?

KEEP

Something embarrassing, like:

- a trendy item of clothing, like parachute pants or teal-blue eye shadow

- a "craze," like a Snuggie or a pet rock

- an entire set, like the pinafores you and your sisters all wore one holiday

TOSS

Something embarrassing, if:

- it doesn't make you say, "I can't believe I ever owned that!"

- it just wouldn't store well

STORAGE SOLUTION

Have a labeled box ready to fill with the keepers to make the process easier. Create one box for each person you want to keep things for. You can give it to them now or save it for later. As you identify items, you can add them to the box. If that person expresses an interest in holding on to something, you can add the item to the box.

KEEP/TOSS CLUE: If your answer to the question "Does this make me happy to see it?" is a yes, then it is most likely a keeper. However, your answer to that question may change over time, so revisit your treasures often.

Ceremonial Clothing

Current clothing, such as you keep in your bedroom closet, is covered in Chapter 5. Here, we will talk about keepsake clothing, from a baby onesie to a wedding dress and everything in between.

KEEP

This ceremonial clothing:

- college graduation gown

- wedding dress

- baptismal gown

TOSS

Ceremonial clothing that:

- hasn't aged well

- you aren't sure for what occasion it was worn, who wore it, or why it was kept

- has become moldy, musty, or mildewed

> ### STORAGE SOLUTION
> ....
> Instead of trying to store the entire article of clothing, consider repurposing some of the pieces. A treasured tuxedo shirt can be made into a funky throw pillow, and a bunch of T-shirts can be made into a quilt. It can be very special to incorporate a piece of a loved one's clothing into your own on your special day. You can opt to save a single strand of lace from a wedding gown instead of the entire gown.

KEEP THIS, TOSS THAT

KEEP
These items from your wedding:

- 1 wedding invitation

- 1 ceremony program

- 1 example of signage, like place cards and table numbers

- guest book

- 1 wedding favor (as long as it isn't perishable)

- copies of speeches by the maid of honor and best man

- ring pillow

- charm or ribbon from your bridal bouquet

- wedding cake topper

- your "something blue"

- earrings or other jewelry you wore

- unity candle or significant altarpiece

TOSS
These items from your wedding:

- excess personalized cocktail napkins and matches

- leftover favors

- dried flowers

- extra programs and printed material, like save-the-date cards

KEEP/TOSS CLUE: Before you toss wedding items from a previous marriage, consider if there is anything you want to share with your children. Sometimes there is something they'd like to keep, like the wedding topper or something to reference during the planning of their own wedding, like the readings you selected.

Most of the joy of keeping a wedding dress comes from being able to try it on or show it off to other people. If you are keeping it, consider having it dry-cleaned, then packing it yourself using acid-free tissue paper and an acid-free box. Store it in a climate-controlled space instead of in the attic, garage, or basement.

9 Ways to Reuse a Wedding Dress

1. A piece of the dress used as someone's "something old"

2. Altered or used as material for a new wedding dress for a future bride

3. Made into a baby blanket

4. Tailored into a christening gown or romper

5. A piece made into a ring-bearer pillow for a future wedding

6. A piece used as a tooth-fairy pillow for your children

7. Used as spare material or altered into a new dress for another special occasion

8. Made into a keepsake quilt, perhaps with pieces of your spouse's wedding-day attire or other special garments

9. Made into a Christmas tree skirt

KEEP/TOSS CLUE: There is no rule that says you can't use personalized napkins after the event has past. Keep one or two, and use the rest.

Household Items

KEEP

Basic household tools that:

- are high-quality and will stand the test of time

- have all their parts and are easy to operate

- are easy to box up and store

- are simple to use, like a spatula

TOSS

Basic household tools that:

- are too trendy, like a green smoothie maker

- are delicate and will probably be damaged in long-term storage

- don't truly fill you with pleasant nostalgia

- meet the criteria for tossing explained in Chapter 2

KEEP/TOSS CLUE: Given a choice, we'd all prefer to get something from our loved ones that we can actually use. A useful item that holds special memories is a total bonus. Something as simple as Mom's kitchen colander may not appear all that special until you realize you think of Mom every time you strain pasta.

KEEP
These types of handwritten notes:

- 1 greeting card per special person to preserve their handwriting/signature

- something that contains an important piece of family history

- 1 mundane shopping to-do list, or a calendar page to show more of the person's personality or routine

TOSS
Handwritten notes that:

- you'd rather forget you once wrote or received

- are school papers noting poor performance or other reprimands

- are practically illegible or too damaged to preserve

KEEP
Family recipes that:

- use common ingredients

- are family favorites

- are the recipes you're "famous" for

TOSS
Family recipes that:

- don't turn out well

- don't have a story behind them

- use uncommon or hard-to-find ingredients, decreasing the likelihood that anyone will make them

KEEP/TOSS CLUE: Food and love are interconnected. From Aunt Millie's brownies to Grandma Mary's stuffing, we all have food associations. Think about the recipe you are "known" for, the recipes you make and take to dinner parties or holiday gatherings. These are the ones you want to keep, and having them in your own handwriting makes them all that more special. Don't forget to make a note of whose recipe it is, where it came from, who makes it, and for what occasions.

Assorted Inherited Items

KEEP

These commonly inherited items:

- address books, until they've been skimmed to collect any data you need

- bank passbooks, until you confirm the accounts have been closed

- check showing payment for an everyday purchase to show cost of inflation

- educational records, including school progress reports

- employment records, including contracts and résumés

- genealogy and family-history charts, narratives, family trees

- graduation, baby, marriage invitations, and announcements

- holiday card list

- income-tax returns, until you are sure the estate is settled

- journals, diaries, ledgers

- military records, including discharge papers, letters, awards

- vital records

KEEP/TOSS CLUE: You are not duty-bound to store items; your home is not a museum or storage facility. Just because a relative used and/or kept an item does not mean you are now required to keep it.

TOSS
These inherited items:

- calendars, once you extract any anniversaries and dates of birth for family members

- canceled checks and check registers after checking for purchases of family heirlooms

- church and club newsletters that don't contain significant family announcements

- insurance policies, once you confirm the policy is no longer in effect

- medical bills and records, after jotting down genealogical information, like diagnosed medical conditions

- news clippings, after checking for news of family

- old bank statements

- receipts with the exception of any receipts for heirlooms, which can be used for appraisal purposes

- travel itineraries and brochures

KEEP/TOSS CLUE: If you keep it and it replaces something you already own, it should not become a duplicate. An inherited dresser should replace your current dresser.

STORAGE SOLUTION

Handheld wand scanners, like the VuPoint Magic Wand Portable Scanner, can scan 3-D items, like lace on a gown or rice that was thrown at a wedding ceremony and much more. You can store the scanned image as a jpeg and let the actual item go; many of these items would deteriorate in storage anyhow, so saving the scanned image actually is the way of keeping the item (and memory) safe.

KEEP/TOSS CLUE: Toss it if someone saved it for you or you saved it for years and the only thing keeping you from letting it go is the thought, How can I toss it now?

4 Guilt-Free Ways to Toss Treasures

1. Instead of saving the entire item, just save a piece, like a snippet of a baby blanket.

2. Take a photograph of the item to preserve the memory without the memento.

3. Sell the items, then donate the proceeds "in memoriam" to your loved one's favorite charity.

4. Donate historical items to a museum, university, or the local historical society.

KEEP/TOSS CLUE: Sometimes a photo can replace the item itself, but other keepsakes need to be felt and touched to truly be appreciated, like your father's smoking pipe that still has a faint scent of tobacco, or an embossed greeting card with your mother's handwriting imprinted on it.

Did you know?

The fewer things you keep, the more special they will be to you.

Collections

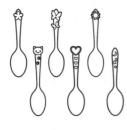

Unless you are thoughtful about which collections you keep, there's a good chance groups of things will take up a considerable amount of valuable space in your home.

Many people report that the joy is in the collecting itself. If that's true for you, then you might consider letting your amassed collection go or pick and choose to keep only the pieces that are really meaningful to you.

For the items you choose to keep, you want to display them so you can enjoy them. A collection you love can't make you happy staying in boxes in the closet. Whenever possible, look for ways to blend the items with your existing decor, like storing a matchbook collection in a tall glass vase and placing it on the sidebar in the dining room.

If you spent a lot of money on your collection and don't want to give away your investment or you have reason to believe the collection is valuable, get more information. Logging onto eBay.com, goantiques.com, or abebooks.com is a quick and easy way to research the monetary value of items. You might be surprised when you find out what the real value is, and if it's less than you expected, it can make tossing a whole lot easier.

Remember, you can consider your collection complete at any point. If you have been gifted another addition to your collection for every holiday and birthday, you can gracefully let loved ones know your collection is complete and you no longer feel the need to add pieces.

Many people would be willing to let all or some of their collection go if they could pass it along to someone who would appreciate it as much as they once did. Check with your local library, or look in the local newspaper for a get-together of people with the interest. Or log onto Meetup.com to search by ZIP code.

Before you toss any part of your collection, take a photo as a reminder.

These are the collectibles that generally hold their value over time. To find more, Google "old things worth money."

1. 1st edition books, signed books, or vintage cookbooks
2. Comic books, especially from the 1930s
3. *TV Guide* with notable figure on the cover
4. Royal Albert china
5. Depression-era glassware
6. New England Glass Company or Boston & Sandwich Glass Company perfume bottles
7. Upside Down Ball Mason jars
8. Precious Moments figurines
9. Retro video games like Atari and Gameboy
10. Out-of-date electronics
11. Vintage Polaroid camera
12. Guitars, especially Fender, Gibson, or Martin
13. 1800s postcards
14. Cereal boxes with a notable figure on the front
15. Character lunch boxes
16. Coca-Cola branded items
17. Mechanical banks
18. Retro or vintage T-shirts
19. Vintage holiday decorations
20. Retro toys, including American Girl, Barbie, Cabbage Patch, and Strawberry Shortcake dolls; Beanie Babies; Easy Bake Ovens; GI Joe, Power Rangers, and Transformers action figures; My Little Pony and Polly Pocket toys; Tamagotchis; and View-masters

KEEP/TOSS CLUE: China and crystal often come in sets, but if you're not hosting fancy dinner parties, these pieces stay boxed up in the attic. If you don't like it and never use it, toss it. If you like it but never use it, consider repurposing. Great-Grandma's fine china teacup can sit on your bedside table to hold your wedding ring as you sleep; a small dish in the vanity drawer can store hair elastics; and old toothpick holders can keep Q-tips upright in the bathroom. Don't be afraid to break up a set if you don't plan on passing it down to future generations.

Did you know?

If you think that old dresser in your attic might be valuable, get it appraised. Find local appraisers at American Society of Appraisers Appraisers.org. Prefer to do some homework on your own? Check out GoAntiques.com or Kovels.com. Or get a price guide from your local library; some libraries even host their own version of an *Antiques Roadshow*–style event.

Chapter 14
Office

No life decluttering project would be complete without a look at the office area. Whether it's a home office, professional office, or mobile office, the goal is the same – keep what you use (or legally need to keep) and toss the rest.

Efficiency is the goal here. Imagine having a working pen at your fingertips instead of having to dig through a drawer. And while a pen might seem like a small thing, when all these little items are organized, your job is less stressful, and you can be more productive.

So yes, we're going to toss the pens (and staplers and rubber bands and all other office supplies) that don't work, the ones you don't like, and the ones you don't need, and we'll keep a reasonable number that still write well.

Ask yourself these key questions:
1. Is it easy to work? Do I know how to work it?
2. When was the last time I used or referenced it?
3. Do I need to stock this many, or can I easily get more when I need it from a central stock room?

Now, let's get to work!

Home Office

KEEP
Writing instruments that:

- are comfortable to hold and use

- have plenty of ink still left inside

- have an intact finger grip to make writing with the pen more comfortable

- highlight without obscuring the text beneath it

- are smear-free to keep the ink under the highlighting legible

TOSS
Writing instruments that:

- have cracked barrels, missing clips, or are otherwise compromised

- are promotional items you picked up for free that are not your favorite go-to pens

- won't write on a variety of surfaces, such as glossy paper

- are in unprofessional colors (you don't want to write a business letter in pink glitter ink)

- are not quick-drying or have been smearing ink

- have an offending odor

- bleed through paper

- have a fraying or mushy tip, making your lines less than smooth

KEEP/TOSS CLUE: When you find yourself constantly skipping over a pen in the drawer or pen cup, that's a clue you need to toss it.

KEEP THIS, TOSS THAT

KEEP

These pieces of office equipment and supplies:

- functioning office equipment like a printer, fax, scanner, copier

- the computer you use all the time

- chargers and cords for equipment you use regularly

TOSS

These pieces of office equipment and supplies:

- broken chargers for electronics

- chargers or cords for equipment you no longer own

- empty printer-ink cartridges and toner containers

- old versions of equipment you upgraded

- outdated lists or sticky notes from your desk or stuck to your computer

- office supplies that are unusable

- mostly used notepads, yellow legal pads, spiral notebooks, or pad-folio holders

- broken label makers and the tape that goes with them

- outdated versions of software and software you never use

- outdated technology, like free-standing answering machines or tape voice recorders

- torn, faded, bent, or otherwise unusable files and folders

- supplies for office machines you no longer own

> ### STORAGE SOLUTION
> ....
> Keep excess office supplies in a box, which will allow you to "shop" without leaving your office.

KEEP

These homework supplies if you have school-age children:

- sharpened pencils with erasers

- pencil sharpener

- colored pencils, pens, and markers

- 2 highlighter pens

- crayons

- ruler

- glue stick

- stapler with a box of staples

- pack of lined, 3-hole-punched, filler paper

- self-stick notepad

- pack of index cards

- large white poster board

- calculator

- timer to track reading time

Homeschooling Essentials

If you homeschool your children, also keep these items:

- Textbooks

- Date stamp to date everyday papers

- "Teacher" marking pen in a noticeable color

- Handheld dry-erase boards

- Library card

- Electric pencil sharpener (mechanical pencils can be too delicate for kids)

TOSS

These items if you have school-age children:

- flashcards below your youngest child's grade level

- too-small pencils

- dried-up markers

- broken backpacks

- crayon nubs

- tests you and they will not refer back to

- notes from school they no longer need to reference

- outdated schedules

- old notes, flyers, reminders, and letters

Scissor Suggestions!

Scissors—you can keep more than one, but just don't run with them. This is one of those useful tools that is often needed in more than one room of the house. It is a waste of time having to walk room to room to locate a pair when needed. Consider keeping pairs:

- in the office
- in the bathroom to open products or trim your bangs
- two in the kitchen (one for opening product packages and one for cutting food like herbs)

- in the garage
- in your sewing basket
- with the gift wrap
- in a bedroom dresser to snip off clothing tags or stray strings

To keep track of which pair belongs where, you can write on the outside of the blade with permanent marker or label them on a piece of tape wrapped around the handle.

Corporate Office

KEEP

These items in your workplace office:

- a dry-erase board to jot down notes (this prevents piles of sticky notes)

- current documents, paper and digital

- important paperwork and files, but mark them with "toss dates" so you know when you can let something go without looking it over again

- just the amount of furniture you need (side chairs tend to collect clutter)

- office equipment in working order

- a few photographs and mementoes to show your style

- current vendor catalogs (6 months or newer) and one year of professional journals (12 months or newer)

- a working label maker with tape, if you use one

- a meeting folder filled with reports, items to be discussed, and items to hand off

- a "waiting for" file filled with notes and reminders for anything you are waiting on from someone else

- one designated work bag to tote items to and from work

KEEP THIS, TOSS THAT

TOSS

These items from your workplace office:

- first drafts, outdated files, and anything you don't need to keep

- anything that doesn't work, is no longer needed, or is the older version of something you've upgraded

- excess knickknacks, plants (real or artificial), and decorations

- outdated vendor catalogs (6 months or older) and old copies of professional journals (12 months or older)

- random stickers used to label files, shelves, and drawers

- scattered notes that make you scramble to find what you need

- reports in multiple drafts that leave you wondering which is the most current

- excess copies of documents you printed out for a meeting

- all the random tote and messenger bags half filled with stuff you never emptied out

- all those reminders you keep everywhere else as the reminder you are waiting for something from someone else

- anything that can otherwise be saved or retrieved from online

- anything that is past its "keep" deadline

Did you know?

The average box of replacement staples for a standard size stapler contains 25,000 staples. You'd have to staple 480 things per week to use up that many staples in a single year! When buying more staples, look for smaller-size boxes. Even if the staples cost a few cents more, it will be money well spent!

KEEP

These five things in your desk drawer:

- black permanent marker, for addressing packages

- mechanical pencils so you can toss the pencil sharpener and pencils that require sharpening

- padded envelopes (2 small, 2 medium, 2 large) so you have one on hand to use and one as backup while you buy a replacement

- ruler

- forever stamps, so you don't have to worry about changes in the postal rate

TOSS

These three things from your desk drawer:

- sticky notes that are too tiny to be functional

- calculator, which is now available on every tablet, computer, and smartphone

- notebooks or pads of paper with just a few blank pages left inside

KEEP

These personal items in your desk drawer:

- adhesive bandages
- breath mints
- compact mirror
- current restaurant delivery menus
- dental floss
- deodorant
- feminine sanitary products
- forever stamps
- hand lotion
- lint roller
- lip balm
- mouthwash
- over-the-counter medication, such as headache medicine
- snacks
- spare phone charger
- umbrella

TOSS

These personal items from your desk drawer:

- almost-empty tubes of lotion or old makeup
- anything that should be but is no longer sterile, like an adhesive bandage that has been opened
- anything that belongs somewhere else but had ended up in the drawer
- crumbling containers of deodorant
- crushed, stale, or expired snacks
- excessive amounts of anything, like two boxes of your favorite tea
- expired over-the-counter medication
- lint rollers with no sticky paper left
- phone charger that doesn't fit your current phone

KEEP

These supplies for your mobile office:

- a flat surface for writing on, such as a clipboard

- a portable file box for hanging files

- breath mints

- brochures (current)

- business cards (current)

- chargers for phone and computer

- tablet/phone stylus, if needed

- reference or "hot" files for current projects

- mini lint roller to de-lint clothes before a meeting

- pens

- rolling case, if needed to tote inventory

- small versions of office supplies, such as staplers and tape

- takeout menus to call ahead for pickup

- travel-size toiletries, like mouthwash and dental floss

TOSS

These supplies for your mobile office:

- business cards that have gotten bent or stained

- old notes

- old versions of your brochures

- pads of paper with only a few sheets left

- files that need to be archived

- dried-up pens and highlighters

STORAGE SOLUTION

Grid-It! by Cocoon is a board covered with elastic straps—just slip in what you want to store, and anything from your lipstick to your phone charger will be held in place!

Chapter 15

Paperwork

If you have a filing cabinet or two so packed with paper that your filing system is now a precariously stacked pile of papers on top of the filing cabinet, you're going to love my alternative methods for filing.

Papers in a box (for everyday papers)
Place a tabletop box in a central location, like the kitchen counter. Add a handful of hanging file folders to the box and adhere sticky notes to the inside back of the file folder, leaving a little sticking up over the edge to create a label you can write on. Make a note on your calendar of time-sensitive papers, like party invitations or bills, before putting them into a file; otherwise, it'll be out of sight, out of mind.

What should go in this box? Bills to be paid, tickets to events, newspaper clippings for things you want to do or places you want to go, recipes, and party invitations. What doesn't go in the box? Magazines, catalogs, your to-read pile, receipts, or financial statements. To keep from outgrowing your box, skim your file tabs weekly to recycle the contents of the ones that are no longer active, like the town recycling schedule from last week.

Papers in a binder (for specific categories of paperwork like medical records or financial accounts)
Fill a three-ring binder with a few pocketed folders and plastic sheet protectors so you can easily slip papers in. Now you can grab your medical binder on your way to a doctor's appointment or take the financial binder when you meet with your advisor. Store these binders someplace handy, like a bookshelf or kitchen cabinet.

Papers in an accordion file (for archival filing)

Label each slot of a twelve-slot accordion file folder with one month of the year and write the year on the outside of the folder. In each slot, place paperwork you most likely won't need but want to be able to locate quickly if you do. This includes things like stubs from bills you've paid, explanation of health-care benefits, banking and credit card statements, receipts, and warranties.

Depending upon the type of paperwork, you may want to keep it up to seven years (check out the Special Feature on page 258 to see exactly when to toss what types of paper). As you fill a year's worth of paper, store the entire accordion file in a plastic tub. After seven years, shred the papers from the file and reuse it.

Papers in safe storage (for difficult-to-replace or irreplaceable documents)

Use a watertight, fire-resistant box that you can store in a discreet spot in your home. Or opt for a bank safe deposit box for items like passports. See page 260 for a complete list of the papers you need to keep forever in this box.

Ask yourself these key questions when considering what paperwork to keep or toss:

1. When I actually use it/refer to it/need it, will the information still be current?
2. Can it easily be duplicated or created if needed again?
3. Can I digitize this easily?

Let's turn those piles into files!

Personal Documents and Records

KEEP

This health and medical-insurance paperwork:

- copies of your medical reports

- a list of your important medical events

- current medication list

- physician referrals

- information sheets that come with prescriptions

TOSS

This health and medical-insurance paperwork:

- physician directories, since an up-to-date version is available online

- duplicates of records

KEEP

These (current) end-of-life documents:

- estate-planning documents

- wills

- trusts

- powers of attorney

- health-care proxy

TOSS

These end-of-life documents:

- drafts or previous versions of final documents

- documents no longer in effect

Did you know?

Because so much of your paperwork includes sensitive personal information, when I say "toss," I really mean "shred." You can find a shred event, or some chain office supply stores offer shredding by the pound. Contact your local municipal department or local library to inquire about upcoming paper shred events.

KEEP

This career and college paperwork:

- current employment contract

- awards, designations, certificates

- annual reviews from current employer (or from the past year if you are currently job-seeking)

- final transcript

- letters of recommendation (dated within the past ten years, unless it is from a well-known person within your industry)

- letters stating exemplary service (dated within the past ten years, unless it states something extra important)

TOSS

This career and college paperwork:

- college course notes from classes you attended a year ago or more

- notes for courses you taught, as long as you have a copy on your computer

- drafts of research papers

- research and notes for lectures you prepared and presented

- handouts of all kinds

- course catalogs for past semesters

- interim reports from work or transcripts from school

KEEP/TOSS CLUE: Instead of printing out paper you then need to file, try to keep as much on the computer as possible. Notes from classes you gave or attended can be kept in digital format instead of printed copies.

KEEP

These automobile records for cars you still own:

- automobile title (in a safe-deposit or disaster-proof box)

- maintenance records

- current registration and proof of insurance (in your car)

- current insurance policy

- purchase records

- for any automobiles you sold privately, keep the bill of sale for three years in your accordion-file system

TOSS

These automobile records:

- titles for cars you no longer own

- expired car registrations

- expired insurance policy after one year or longer (kept to prove coverage in the event of late claims)

- expired insurance cards

KEEP

Instruction manuals and warranties for:

- items you still own

- the life of warranty

TOSS

Instruction manuals and warranties for:

- items you no longer own

- items no longer under warranty

- items you already know how to work

- items that you prefer to look up online when you have questions

---

Did you know?

It's a good idea to create an inventory of the items that are in your safe-deposit box. Make a list of what's in the box, write down its location, and keep it all with your keys. For quick reference, keep photocopies at home of documents stored in the box.

How Long Do I Really Need to Keep This Paperwork?

Keep 90 days

- ATM and bank deposit withdrawal slips

- credit card bill (unless required to support a tax return or for a warranty or to prove that repairs or maintenance was done on something you might sell)

- receipts for valuable items, such as jewelry, electronics, and art (unless originals are required by your insurance carrier)

- investment statements

- utility bills

Did you know?

You can digitize papers using the apps CamScanner or Microsoft OfficeLens.

Keep 1 year (if you have multiples, keep the year-end one)

- bank brokerage statements

- bank statements (unless you need them to support a tax filing)

- proof of casualty or theft losses like a police report or insurance claim

- charitable donation receipts (unless you need them to support a tax filing)

- proof of gambling losses and wins for tax reporting purposes, like wagering tickets, canceled checks or credit records, and receipts from the gambling facility

- health benefit information

- homeowner or rental property expenses like maintenance receipts

- insurance (until you renew the policy)

- interest statements

- investment statements

- mortgage statements

- receipts for reimbursable work expenses

- donated property inventory receipt proving donation confirmation

- retirement account statements

- student loan statements

- tax preparation costs

- paycheck stubs until you get your W2

- undisputed medical bills (keep for one year after they've been paid)

Keep 7 years

- 1099

- real estate tax forms and records

- tax returns and supporting documents

- W2

- medical bills and statements

- year-end investment statements (keep for at least three years after you sell the investments)

Keep newest version or the year-end summary

- annual insurance policy statements

- Social Security statements

- year-end retirement fund statements

Keep until...

- car, bike or other vehicle records and repair/maintenance receipts (until you sell or donate the vehicle)

- contracts (until the contract is over plus 3 years)

- credit card statements (until paid unless it relates to a tax filing)

- home purchase and improvement records (until you sell the home plus 3 years)

- loan documents (until you sell the item the loan was for)

- real estate deeds (until you sell the property)

- safe deposit box inventory and key (until you give it up)

- warranties and related receipts (until the warranty expires)

Keep forever

- academic records, such as diplomas, final transcripts, and portfolio work

- adoption papers

Did you know?

If more than 25 percent of income was omitted from a tax return, the IRS has six years to challenge your return. This applies only when you can prove you filed an income tax return. Always check with your tax professional to ensure you are keeping what you need but not storing unnecessary papers.

- advance directives, such as your living will and durable power of attorney

- annual statements from your brokerage or other confirmation of investment sales and purchases

- bank account and credit card numbers and log-in information if you access online

- baptismal certificates

- bar/bat mitzvah and bris certificates

- car title(s)

- cemetery plot deeds

- citizenship and immigration paperwork

- copies of your driver's license, green card, passport, and other forms of ID

- CPA audit reports

- current household inventory with assigned values for significant items

- current contact information of family, friends, brokers, agents, doctors, lawyers, and accountants

- death certificates

- documentation of your retirement plan trusts, or stocks, along with beneficiary designations

- employment records

- insurance policies (life, health, long-term care, home, car)

- income tax returns and payment checks

- legal papers (such as divorce decrees, property settlements, contracts, patents, or copyrights)

- life insurance policy
- living trust
- marriage certificates and licenses
- medical and family health history
- military records, including discharge paperwork
- mortgage or loan discharge paperwork
- ownership records (such as real estate deeds and stock certificates)

- passports
- photo negatives and one wedding and baby photo
- PIN numbers for cash accounts
- retirement and pension records
- Social Security cards
- wills

Did you know?

It's possible to replace some important documents. Here's how:

Birth certificate—Go to cdc.gov/nchs/w2w.htm and click on the state you were born in

Social Security card—Social Security Administration: socialsecurity.gov

Passport—U.S. Department of State: Travel.State.gov

Diploma or school transcripts—Contact your school's registrar

Tax returns—Internal Revenue Service: irs.gov

Car title—Contact your state's motor vehicle department or dmv.org

Property deed—Contact the county clerk's office

Financials

KEEP
This financial and investment paperwork:

- pay stubs

- canceled checks for the past twelve months

- deposit and withdrawal slips until account is reconciled

- monthly bank and credit card account statements (for seven years, if tax-related purchases on statements)

- annual bank and credit card account statements

- investment statements and trade confirmations

- dividend payment statements

- defined-benefit plan documents

- letters that confirm your right to a future retirement benefit, such as an employer's pension plan

- savings bonds

- household furnishings paperwork, like the bill of sale for a piece of artwork or your dining-room set

- household inventory list

- receipts and warranties for large purchases, such as your refrigerator, television, or washing machine

- current appraisals on home and items on inventory list

KEEP/TOSS CLUE: Keep seven years' worth of business-related backup documents to support your tax returns, like final budgets, receipts, and contracts. You can toss non-tax-related items such as old conference materials, first drafts of final documents, and outdated business cards and brochures.

- receipts pertaining to home improvements, since these will be needed for calculating the capital gains on the sale of your home

TOSS
This financial and investment paperwork:

- pay stubs, on a yearly basis once you've matched them to your annual W-2 statement

- bank slips after proper credits and withdrawals have been confirmed

- monthly or quarterly bank and credit card account statements, once the annual statement has been received and confirmed correct

- fund prospectuses

- disclosures paperwork

- brochures for insurance or investments

- additional offers or solicitations from your financial institutions

- paper versions of anything you have saved on the computer or have access to online

- old or outdated appraisals

- purchase receipts for art, antiques, collectibles if you no longer own the item, plus one year past the sale of the item

KEEP
These insurance policies:

- auto, homeowners, liability: as long as the statute of limitations runs in the event of late claims, plus one year

- disability, medical, life, personal property, umbrella: for the life of the policy, plus one year

TOSS
These insurance policies and related items:

- expired insurance cards

- policies for covered property you no longer own

- expired term life policies

- canceled or otherwise ended coverage

Paperwork for Children with Special Needs

If your child has been diagnosed as having special needs, you know the overwhelming amount of paperwork that you need to process. Keep your paperwork organized by filing the current papers in a travel file tote. This is an easy way to have it handy to grab and take with you to appointments, meetings, and therapy sessions.

Fill a portable file box with about twenty hanging file folders. Your files will be personalized to your needs, but here are some suggested categories:

- contact information (for all the people you meet who you might want to connect with)

- master providers list

- current medications list

- websites/online resources

- therapy tracker

- conversations (a place to keep the notes during conversations to keep all the information straight)

- school (individual education plan—IEPs—and assessments)

- medical insurance/billing records

- psychological evaluations

- speech/language evaluations

- diagnosis letters

- progress notes

- support groups

- associations/organizations (that have information that can help you or ones that you volunteer your time for)

KEEP

- a single calendar specific to tracking appointments, bill due dates, and insurance notes

- original diagnosis letters

- business cards for current providers and places

TOSS

- appointment reminders for past appointments

- brochures, pamphlets, and booklets

- research and other information you printed from online (once you've read it)

- old directions

- event flyers and mailings

STORAGE SOLUTION

Color coding categories is an easy way to tell files apart. Try primary-colored files, which are easy to replace if you run out. Use a different color for medical, education, psychology, therapy, and medical insurance files.

KEEP

Bills that:

- are current and need to be paid

- your most recent bill paid until you confirm proper credit from your last payment

TOSS

These items that typically accompany your bills:

- return envelopes (unless you pay via check and will use them)

- promotional inserts

KEEP

Receipts for everyday purchases until:

- you confirm the transaction has cleared your account in the proper amount

- you're sure you won't return the item

- you've confirmed if you need it for insurance valuation

- 30 days after purchase, if the store offers a price-matching policy

- 1 year after the sale of your home (for home improvements and repairs)

- 7 years after purchase, if you deduct for business or expense-report purposes

- the warranty and any extended coverage you purchased expires

TOSS

Receipts from:

- grocery trips, once the food has been consumed

- clothing after the length of the return policy

- any item, once the warranty term has expired or you no longer own it

---

Did you know?

Most stores will price-match your purchase within 30 days, as long as you are able to prove your purchase with the receipt.

Everyday Papers and Junk Mail

KEEP

The following everyday papers:

- invitations for events you either need to RSVP to or you've confirmed your attendance

- travel brochures and day-trip ideas

- credit offers or credit-limit increase offers you plan to take advantage of

- store flyers you want to make the time to read

- current sports schedules, recycling calendars, and event calendars

- a list of books you want and intend to read

- tickets to upcoming events and newspaper clippings of upcoming ideas

- party-planning notes, invite lists, and menu ideas for upcoming gatherings

- gift ideas for the current season: ideas of gifts to buy for others or a wish list for yourself, pictures clipped from catalogs stapled to the order information

If you have school-age children, also keep these everyday papers:

- lunch tickets

- current school and extracurricular activity schedule(s)

- current flyers and reminders, until they have been transferred onto the calendar

- schoolwork in progress

- recent homework to use as a study guide

Kitchen Paperwork

The refrigerator can quickly turn into a bulletin board of paperwork precariously tacked on by magnets. This is not an ideal scenario, especially when the papers tumble off and slide under the fridge. Take down the papers—there is a better way! Everything you keep on your fridge can be better managed with my "Life in a box" system. If you get a lot of takeout, you might also consider storing a binder devoted to menus in a kitchen cabinet or on a nearby bookshelf.

TOSS
From the front of the fridge:

- announcements

- business cards

- calendars and schedules

- coupons

- flyers

- invites

- magnets

- memos

- photos

- recipes

- takeout menus

KEEP
Takeout menus that are:

- for restaurants you still order from

> **KEEP/TOSS CLUE:** Store an extra set of the most commonly used takeout menus in your car for those evenings when you are already out and need to place an order for pickup.

TOSS

Takeout menus that are:

- for restaurants that you now exclusively order from online

- for restaurants you no longer like

- for restaurants no longer in existence

- totally out of date

- duplicates of the same menu

KEEP

Coupons for:

- brands you actually use

- products you really need to purchase

- stores you plan to shop at before the coupon expires

- something you were already going to buy

TOSS

Coupons that:

- are expired or will be expired by the time you make it to that store

- you are holding on to just because it is a great deal, but you don't really need the items

- are for products you already own

- are for items that you wouldn't use before they expire

STORAGE SOLUTION

Staple or paper-clip any coupons for a restaurant directly to their takeout menu (if you have one), so you are more likely to remember to use them the next time you place an order.

STORAGE SOLUTION

Frequently referenced items, like schedules or a go-to recipe, are best tacked on the inside of a top kitchen cabinet or pantry door.

TOSS
These everyday papers:

- mailings from organizations you no longer belong to

- glossy ads for sales you won't be shopping

- store flyers you aren't visiting this week

- offers you are not interested in

- old grocery lists

- completed to-do lists

- invitations for events that have passed or you will not be attending

- to-be-shredded pile of papers (including preapproved credit offers)

- random phone numbers written on scraps of paper without a name

- driving directions you printed and no longer need

- brochures and pamphlets you might reference in the future that are now available online

---

Did you know?

You can significantly reduce the amount of junk mail you receive with just a few clicks and calls. CatalogChoice.org will have your name removed from unwanted catalog mailing lists at no cost. You can stop the unsolicited credit card offers by going to OptOutPreScreen.com or calling 888-5-OPT-OUT. And the easiest way to reduce the amount of junk mail you receive, by up to 70 percent, is to register with DMAchoice.org. Also, there's a great phone app called PaperKarma (learn more at PaperKarma.com).

Chapter 16
Digital Life

All the digital clutter—files that don't take up "real" space—can still take a real toll on you. Your e-mail inbox with thousands of e-mails, an e-reader crammed with downloaded books you'll never read, and all those forgotten photos waiting in your phone. Unless you get a "limited storage" alert, it can be tempting to just keep them all!

But a cluttered virtual desktop is as bad as the top of your actual desk being covered with clutter. Think about how much time it wastes to locate the one e-mail or photograph among all those digital files. Going forward, keeping your technology clutter-free comes down to having a few simple routines in place like downloading photos at the end of a trip and renaming the files so they are searchable.

Ask yourself these key questions:
1. Do I have access to this because it is stored elsewhere or can easily be found in an online search?
2. Do I still have the technology to view this file?
3. Do I have a newer version of this file?

Are you ready to toss some of those digital files? Here's some suggestions about what to keep and what to delete!

Computer Files

KEEP
These computer and electronic files:

- desktop icons you click on often

- bookmarked sites and favorites you still reference

- folders named for what is inside, like "Insurance Documents," not the generic "My Documents"

- a folder named "Archive," where you can store documents you are pretty sure you can get rid of but aren't quite ready to delete for good

- a simple, clean, beautiful desktop background

TOSS
These computer and electronic files:

- old files you now have a final or more updated version of

- downloads you no longer need

- the files you saved on your desktop to keep within sight while you were working on them but you no longer need

- files you no longer reference, like last year's sporting schedule or a letter you already printed and mailed but don't need to keep

- programs you no longer use

- multiple toolbars that are redundant or for functions you don't use

- cookies, cache, and browser history

- apps you no longer use

- shortcuts to documents or programs that you no longer need or use

- RSS subscriptions you no longer want

- a busy desktop wallpaper or background

KEEP THIS, TOSS THAT

KEEP
Downloaded books that:

- are on subjects you are currently interested in

- you will make time to read

- are excellent reference books, where it makes sense to read it in book format rather than searching for the topic online

TOSS
Downloaded books that:

- you've already read and will not reread

- you will never get around to reading

- you thought you wanted to read but soon realized you didn't love and never got past the first few pages

- you downloaded for the simple fact that it was free but really have no interest in reading

KEEP/TOSS CLUE: Unfortunately, the fine print often prohibits you from donating or gifting e-books and apps, so don't feel bad about deleting them from your device.

Downloads & DVR Recordings

KEEP

- Podcasts you enjoy and need to have downloaded because you won't have WiFi when you want them

- PDF files like restaurant menus you refer to all the time

- DVR recordings that you have not watched but absolutely will

- Notes and memos that still hold relevant information

TOSS

- Podcasts you already listened to or can stream when you want them

- PDF files like directions you won't refer to again or can access as needed

- Audiobooks you listened to, won't replay, or did not enjoy and won't finish

- Notes and memos that have outdated information on them

- DVR recordings for shows that can be watched on demand or through a streaming service

Did you know?

Before donating phones or computers, it is highly recommended that you wipe them clean of your personal data—which might be as simple as resetting the device to its original factory settings.

E-mail and Social Media

KEEP
E-mails that:

- contain information you'll need to reference again, like a receipt from online shopping

- are about something you need to take action on or follow up on

TOSS
E-mails that:

- are electronic newsletters you signed up for but don't make time to open and read

- you no longer have an interest in reading

- are coupons, sales, and flyers you aren't interested in

- are automatically generated notifications via e-mail from sites such as Facebook or Yahoo groups

- are e-mail reminders, like a bill-pay notice that is no longer current

KEEP/TOSS CLUE: You can toss junk e-mail messages by marking them as such so future messages from the same sender are automatically diverted from your Inbox into your Junk or Spam folder. Each e-mail provider has its own way of doing this, so check the Help feature on yours to find out how.

KEEP

The following in your social media accounts:

- Facebook friends you like receiving updates from

- Facebook page likes whose updates show up in your news feed

- Twitter feeds for only the Tweets that interest you

- Tweets from people you still find interesting, funny, or helpful

- your Pinterest pinboards that are still relevant to you

- others' Pinterest pinboards that you want to make the time to view

- photos on social-sharing sites that you still like or find flattering

- LinkedIn connections with just the people you want to stay in contact with

- Following people on Instagram that post things you like to follow

- Subscriptions to YouTube channels that post videos you like to watch

TOSS

The following from your social media accounts:

- Facebook friends who share updates you are not interested in or prefer not to see

- Pinterest boards you no longer wish to follow

- any groups or pages you never visit, are not active on, or are no longer interested in keeping up to date with

- Instagram friends that post things that you are no longer interested in

- Subscriptions to YouTube channels that post videos you no longer care about

- Pins that are unattainable and make you feel bad

Did you know?

You can register for free with Unroll.me to unsubscribe with one click from all those e-mail newsletters you opted into over the years but no longer wish to receive.

Smartphones

KEEP

The following items on your smartphone:

- texts you need to store for personal reasons (lock them to prevent yourself from accidently deleting them)

- running lists of restaurants you want to eat at and books you want to read

- a list of current clothing and shoe sizes for people you buy for

- an ICE (in case of emergency) entry in your contacts list—this is the number emergency personnel will search your phone for in case you can't call yourself

- a snapshot of the numbered sign near your car in the parking lot so you can locate it again or spot the number if you need to pay at a parking meter

- when traveling, a picture of the contents of your suitcase in case it is lost and you need to make an insurance claim, also a picture of the suitcase so you can show customer service what bag you are looking for

- photos for future reference, like the label of the delicious bottle of wine you just shared, a cute haircut you'd like to show your stylist, the bag of food your dog prefers to eat, or an ink cartridge you need to pick up so you don't forget which model, style, or kind

- a photo of any outfit you are trying to find a piece to match so when you are in the store, you can refer to the photo to see if the new piece will work

TOSS

These items from your smartphone:

- photos that have already been transferred to another device for safekeeping

- voice mails you already listened to and no longer need to refer to

- old or no-longer-needed contacts from the address book

- apps you've downloaded but never access

- photos that are not flattering or that you don't know why you took or kept

---

18 Phone Numbers to Keep Handy

You should keep this contact information handy in case you need to make a call but have no way to look up the number (for instance, if you lose power or have no Internet access).

1. Your doctor (and your child's pediatrician)
2. Hospital
3. After-hours emergency-care center
4. The American Association of Poison Control Centers' national emergency hotline: (800) 222-1222
5. Vet (if you have pets)
6. Animal hospital (if you have pets)
7. Gas company
8. Electric company
9. Water company
10. Alarm company (if your house is alarmed)
11. Locksmith
12. Towing company
13. Local police department number for nonemergency
14. American Red Cross
15. Federal Emergency Management Agency (FEMA)
16. Phone numbers of neighbors, family, and friends living close by
17. School numbers (if you have kids)
18. Mom and dad's office/cell phone numbers

Chapter 17
Clutter Challenges

Despite all your efforts to tidy up, sometimes clutter is unavoidable. Many life events, some happy, some sad, can play havoc not only with your emotions but with your stuff. There are five main categories of these special clutter challenges:

1. Change in housing: Whether across town or across country, there's nothing like a move to force you to pare down. But moving can also create extra paperwork, and it can be so overwhelming, you're tempted to just dump everything in boxes without sorting.

2. Loss of a loved one: During the painful time of grieving, the last thing you may feel like doing is sorting through your loved one's belongings. Prepare yourself in advance for the memories and emotions that may come flooding in, and don't forget to check your loved one's will to make sure you

honor any special designations he or she wanted to make.

3. Getting your affairs in order: To avoid passing the burden of sorting your clutter onto your loved ones, organize your paperwork and pare down your belongings for those left behind to manage your estate. Document any stories about special pieces like household furnishing, souvenirs, artwork, and jewelry, and send some items home with family now.

4. Change in living arrangements: Whether you are getting married or divorced, welcoming a new baby or sending your kids off to college, merging households (or separating them) is all about choosing the best of duplicates and keeping only what is needed.

5. Change in ability: If you are injured,

ill, or recovering, or find yourself anxious or depressed, not only do you not feel like yourself, but the clutter problem is compounded by all the insurance paperwork and medical supplies. You also may be extra-busy with doctor appointments or therapy sessions. Be patient with yourself.

6. Change in storage options: If you've been keeping an outside storage unit, now is the time to empty it and reclaim the monthly fee. After every sorting session, take things out of the unit to their destination. Some charitable organizations will pick up directly at your unit. And sometimes you do need to store things outside your home; for instance, you may need to store dorm room items over summer break or home furnishings during a renovation. Just make sure it's temporary and you're only storing things you'll definitely use again when the time is up.

If you are faced with one of these situations, the following Keep/Toss Checklists might help you navigate this stressful time in your life. During these transitional times, ask yourself these key questions:

1. What's the worst thing that could happen if I don't keep this?
2. Can someone else use this now?
3. Would I rather have this or the space it is taking up?

Also, give yourself the gift of saying "yes" when others offer help. Now, get ready for your new normal!

Change in Housing

KEEP

These items for a smooth move:

- a three-ring moving binder filled with all your notes and important paperwork like a moving checklist and contact information for your Realtor and moving company so you can find it in the whirlwind of the move

- a measuring tape for measuring items to see if they will work in the new space

- a floorplan with dimensions of the new space when deciding if larger pieces like artwork and furniture will fit

- photos and/or video of the home's interior and exterior, including favorite rooms and views from the kitchen window to remember the house by

- photos of items as you pack them as an inventory, a great thing to have for insurance purposes

- a photo of the back of electronics as a guide for how to plug them in once you are in the new home

- a recording of you showing and telling the story behind sentimental items that can't be taken to the new home

- just the things that fit the vision you have for this new chapter in your life

TOSS

These items from the old home:

- address labels with your old address

- furniture and decor that don't fit in the new space

- things you won't need in the new space (for example, if you will no longer have a lawn, toss your lawnmower)

- anything that you do not want to spend time cleaning or maintaining in the new space

Did you know?

These are the essentials you should pack in a moving day box, so you'll have them ready when you arrive at your new home:

- bath towels
- bed linens
- change of clothes
- cleaning supplies
- coffeemaker and mugs
- corded phone (the battery in the cordless may need time to recharge)
- eating and cooking utensils
- first-aid kit
- flashlight
- medication and vitamins
- nightlights
- paper products
- personal items (toothbrush, soap, contact lens solution)
- reading glasses
- tool kit
- trash bags

KEEP
These items from the boxes it's taken you months to unpack:

- items that you need but just haven't unpacked yet
- belongings that you really can use
- things that you have room for and like enough to keep

TOSS
These items from the boxes it's taken you months to unpack:

- anything you replaced
- items you regret having moved
- anything that broke during the move (after resolving any pending insurance claims)
- things that don't work in the new space
- stuff still boxed from the move one year later

KEEP

This paperwork related to the purchase/sale of the house:

- addenda, amendments, riders

- affidavit of occupancy

- buyer's agreement

- closing disclosure

- home inspection report(s)

- HUD-1 settlement statement

- initial escrow statement

- loan estimate

- mortgage instrument

- notice of right to rescind

- property deed

- purchase agreement

- seller's disclosure

- state- or government-mandated documents

- title insurance policy

TOSS

This paperwork related to the purchase/sale of the house:

- amortization schedule (which can be easily found online)

- brochures for the title and mortgage companies

- business cards for people or companies you did not use

- duplicate or triplicate copies

- preapproval documents (once approved, you won't need to show them)

Loss of a Loved One

KEEP

These items that belonged to your loved one:

- clothes, shoes, and jewelry that fit you and you would wear

- photographs (see page 223)

- paperwork and documents related to the estate (see page 237)

- collections that you'd like to keep and maintain

- a memento like their pillowcase, something they wrote, or articles of clothing that can be sewn into a memorial quilt or stuffed bear

- furniture, decor, or anything else you like more than yours (just be sure to toss yours) and that will fit in your house

TOSS

These items that belonged to your loved one:

- love letters not addressed to you (unless the person granted you permission to read them)

- anything personal, private, or embarrassing, like a journal

- clothing, shoes, and jewelry you don't need or won't wear

- collections that you are not interested in maintaining

- old documents (see page 238)

- anything they would have thrown out if they were still here

- stashes of everyday things like cardboard boxes or rinsed-out yogurt containers

- anything broken, not in working order, missing pieces, or needing repair

KEEP THIS, TOSS THAT

Getting Your Affairs in Order

KEEP

These items to make things easier for your loved ones to sort your things:

- legal and financial documents (see page 225)

- a list of where to find important things like the key to a safety deposit box and important legal and financial documents

- a note of secret hiding places that people may overlook

- a box labeled "do not open—throw away" to store personal and sensitive items that you do not want other people to see or sort through

- a box for each person you want to give something to

- special occasion stuff that is still good enough to enjoy, like a fine wine

TOSS

These items you don't want to burden your loved ones with:

- anything rotting, broken, or missing parts

- anything that might be unsafe in the future, like a recalled booster seat

- things that will be upgraded, making this older version obsolete

Did you know?

You can authorize your doctors, lawyer, or insurance company to speak with a trusted friend or family member in the event you want that person to assist you in dealing with health or legal issues or insurance claims. Permission usually needs to be given in writing, so inquire about any forms you need to sign and return. This is different from a power of attorney, and you can revoke access at any time.

When Your Family No Longer Wants the Family Heirlooms

It's heartbreaking to know a piece you lovingly cared for may not stay in the family. Whether it is your grandmother's thimble collection or your father's vintage record player, it's special to you because it connects you to the past. So when your children, grandchildren, nieces, and nephews show no interest in your treasures, it can feel like a crushing rejection of your heritage.

Understand that the younger generation may have a different philosophy about this stuff. Just because they don't want the physical items doesn't mean they don't value the stories behind them. If this is the case, take the time now to capture the stories: Write them down, take a video of yourself telling the stories of each object, or invite your loved ones over to tell them the stories in person. Then, try these methods of "tossing" the actual things (also, see Chapter 13 and Appendix B):

- Ask loved ones to "shop" your home, choosing objects they will treasure.

- Use the stuff. If Mom's good teapot gets chipped, at least it served its purpose. And if you don't need a teapot, hang it from a tree in the backyard as a birdfeeder.

- Give the item a big send-off! Dance to your wedding song wearing your wedding dress one more time (even if it won't zip all the way up).

- Match your things with someone outside your family who will treasure them. Perhaps you have a friend, neighbor, or coworker who would appreciate your model train collection more than your kids will.

- Donate your belongings to a cause you believe in. It could bring you happiness to think of a lace tablecloth handmade by your ancestors being used on a table at a senior center.

Keep in mind these pieces are just stuff. The memories are not lost when the item is tossed.

Change in Living Arrangements

KEEP

These items when you are moving in with a new spouse, partner, or roommate:

- an agreed-upon number of "keeps" per person

- the best of any duplicate items (if you can't mutually agree on which is best, toss both and buy new)

- what you both agree is needed

- what works best to blend your two styles

TOSS

These items when you are moving in with a new spouse, partner, or roommate:

- duplicate or triplicate appliances, furniture, or other items

- things from a past love or life (refer to Chapter 13 for guidelines on how to choose just a few keepsakes from the past)

KEEP

These items when you are divorcing or breaking up with a spouse or partner you have been living with:

- any memorabilia to pass along to children

- items that remind you of good times

- divorce decree and other related paperwork (see page 260)

TOSS

These items when you are divorcing or breaking up with a spouse or partner you have been living with:

- anything with a negative memory attached to it

- love letters that no longer have the same meaning

- gifts from your ex-partner

- souvenirs of trips you took with your ex-partner

KEEP

These items when you welcome a new baby:

- clothing (12 onesies, 10 undershirts, 8 pajamas, 3 wide-brimmed hats)

- crib and mattress that meet current safety standards

- fitted mattress sheets, swaddling blankets, and burp cloths

- baby book or calendar to mark milestones

- bouncer or swing

- car seat that meets current safety standards

- fragrance- and dye-free laundry detergent

- hands-free baby carrier and/or stroller

- keepsakes (see page 227)

- baby care products (like shampoo, lotion, nasal aspirator, no-touch digital thermometer)

- toys and activity pieces they will use when age appropriate

TOSS

These items when you welcome a new baby:

- baby care products (like shampoo or lotion) that is irritating to the baby, has too strong a scent, or you have other concerns about

- outgrown items (clothing or toys) that you will not use again

- monogrammed or personalized items if they are not right for you

- anything you can't clean properly

- anything that has been recalled

- baby food processor (a small kitchen one is a less cute version you probably already own)

- bottle sterilizer and bottle warmer

- diaper bags that are too small, too heavy, too large, or otherwise don't work for your needs

KEEP

These items when your child heads off to school or moves out:

- anything they've determined to be a treasure

- anything that fits into a predetermined space (such as two plastic treasure tubs)

- anything they will still use when they come home to visit

- anything they want to save for their career or future children

TOSS

These items when your child heads off to school or moves out:

- anything they have outgrown or deemed too childish

- any keepsakes they have agreed to let go or that don't fit into a predetermined space

- textbooks, class notes, papers, and reports

KEEP THIS, TOSS THAT

Change in Ability

KEEP

These items related to your condition:

- current medications along with instructions noting the dosages, times, side effects, and other helpful information

- medication schedule

- contact information for physicians and testing sites

- medical records, reports, and lab work

- calendar of doctor, therapy, and other appointments

- notes from appointments and lists of questions to ask

- medical supplies (such as gauze, bandages, and catheters) that are still sterile and in good condition

- weights, bands, or other accessories needed

- medical equipment like a walker, cane, crutches, sling

- health insurance information including policy numbers, explanation of benefits forms, and notes from talking with insurance companies (see page 255)

- articles, books, and notes from your own research about your condition

- meal plans

- physical therapy or exercise charts

- emergency card for medical personnel in the event of an emergency

TOSS
These items that won't help your condition:

- outdated medications

- outdated meal plans or physical therapy or exercise charts

- any pamphlets, brochures, articles, or books that do not apply to you or that you do not find helpful

- rehab supports like wedge pillows you are no longer using

- postsurgery supplies like a basin or water pitcher

- bandages and supplies in large quantities you can't use before they go bad

- empty prescription bottles once your personal information has been removed

Change in Storage Options

KEEP

These items if you are clearing out a storage space you have been renting:

- a regular schedule of time to work on the task

- clearly labeled areas of things to sell, donate, trash, recycle, or take home (and remember that if you bring something home, something else has to go)

- things you can take home without overcrowding your space

TOSS

These items if you are clearing out a storage space you have been renting:

- things you already replaced, forgetting you had stored it

- items that will cost you more to move and store than it would to repurchase

- anything that has become outdated while in storage

- items that were damaged or broken while in storage (after any claims have been resolved if the item was insured or the damage was the fault of the facility)

- any guilt associated with the money already spent on the monthly rental

---

Did you know?

Not all homeowners or rental insurance policies cover items that are stored off site. Check with your insurance carrier to see if you need to purchase additional insurance for your items.

When You've Been the Storage Space for Someone Else

You were kind enough to give up your space to house items that do not belong to you, perhaps for a friend or an adult child who has moved out. If you no longer want to be a storage unit, you have the right to ask the owner(s) to collect their stuff. Hopefully, they will be considerate and pick up their items in a timely fashion. If not, try to find out why they are resistant to gathering their stuff. Typically, it is for one of these four reasons:

1. They don't care about what they left behind. If they no longer want the stuff, ask for their permission in writing to sell, donate, use, or toss what they left.

2. They can't transport it. If you need help moving a heavy item, ask friends or family to help or hire a moving company. Renting or borrowing a truck or SUV might solve the problem. It may not be fair for you to incur the cost to get it moved, but at least you won't have to store it any longer.

3. They don't have a place to take it. Help the owner brainstorm where the stuff can go, whether it's a storage unit or another family member or friend.

4. They don't remember what's there. Create an inventory to help the owner make decisions about what they want to do with the stuff. With their permission, you can take photos, a video, or do a live video chat with them, showing them the contents of the bins and boxes.

KEEP

These items if you need temporary storage:

- items you are willing to pay monthly to store but not use

- an inventory of the contents with a diagram of what is stored where

- belongings that your homeowner's insurance policy covers when stored off site

TOSS

These items from your temporary storage:

- things you'll forget about once you put them in storage

- anything that would be less expensive to repurchase

- items that will go out of style by the time you reclaim them from storage

- anything that might be damaged in storage

Did you know?

These items might be illegal to keep or could get damaged in storage.
If you are unsure, always ask for guidelines from the storage facility.

- antique or wooden furniture
- artwork
- cash
- collections (coin, comic, stamp)
- electronics
- firearms or weapons
- fireworks or other explosives
- food and other perishables (including alcohol)
- hazardous items like corrosive, combustible, or flammable chemicals (including propane and paint)
- heirlooms and photographs
- leather products
- live plants or fertilizer
- medications
- musical instruments
- vinyl records
- wine

Conclusion

Congratulations! You did it! Are you doing the declutter dance with me? Let's celebrate all your success together. It has been a real pleasure spending this time with you. I hope our conversation doesn't end here! Pop over to JamieNovak.com now to get even more ideas or take a moment to share your successes with me.

Going forward, you may find these three essential keep/toss rules helpful:

1. Make keep/toss a routine, not a one-time event. Pick one day of the week to be your toss day.

2. Have a toss action plan in place. Once you make the decision to let it go, take the next step to get it out of your house. And please stop bringing so many things home with you.

3. Qualify your keepers. Why are you keeping it, where will you store it, and will you remember you own it in a few months?

What's Your Why?

Initially, your reason for getting organized might be to find something you lost or to tidy things for guests, but once you've done that, you'll need something more to keep the momentum going. Let's look at some of the ways clutter may be affecting you. Once you identify why you'd like to declutter, you can create a mantra to recite because you have better things to do than sort stuff!

You want more time.

- You're done wasting time hunting for things you lost in your house.

- You spend too much time sorting things.

- You're frustrated that everyday tasks, including cleaning, take longer because you have to work around piles of stuff.

You want more money.

- You've wasted money buying organizing solutions like baskets and bins or renting a storage unit.

- You're out the money you spent replacing misplaced items or rebuying things you forgot you already owned.

- It kills you that you've missed costly deadlines like paying late fees on bills because you couldn't find the payment slip, forgetting to return items for a refund or credit by the expiration date (or being unable to do so because you lost the receipt), or losing out on rebates and coupons you forget to file.

You want more energy.

- Just thinking about clutter overwhelms you, zapping your energy.

- You exert energy dealing with the stuff, moving it, and sorting through it.

- You spend energy arguing with your spouse, your kids, your roommate, or your parents about what to do with all the stuff.

You want more space.

- It feels like the clutter is weighing you down.

- Storage spaces are packed with delayed decisions, things you put there just until you're able to go through them.

- You can't use things, like a chair, without moving stuff.

You want more mental clarity.

- Physical clutter can distract you; your mind wanders, thinking about items that catch your eye, making it difficult to stay on task.

- Feeling present may be difficult if you are always faced with leftovers from things you used in the past or faced with items you are planning to use in the future.

- You are forgetful because your mental bandwidth is being monopolized by thoughts like finding your misplaced car keys or trying to remember to pay a bill on time.

You want more confidence.

- You feel like you're the only one with too much stuff, and you feel guilty for letting it get this bad.

- You are embarrassed to let anyone see how you keep your house.

- You compare yourself to others who seem more capable of being organized.

You want more control.

- It feels like your belongings are controlling you instead of you controlling them.

- You don't know what you own or where to find it when you need it.

- You wish you had the freedom that comes with owning less and having less to care for.

Mantra: I want to declutter so I can _____.

Toss These Clutterbug Excuses

Keep your eye on your goal, and let go of all those justifications for keeping clutter.

1. "But what if..."

"What if I need it someday?" Tell yourself: You have what you need; you can't prepare for every unknown. Stay focused on who you are today and how you enjoy spending your time. Keep items that work for you today, an extra few (but not an extra closetful) just in case, and then let the rest go.

2. "But I don't have time to decide now."

If it's not now, then most likely it's never. Resist the urge to shove it in a closet or the garage. Tell yourself: Take care of it now, and you'll never have to think about it again.

3. "But it was expensive."

That high-end green juice maker you had to have but now find too time consuming to clean. Tell yourself: No matter what it is, the money is spent. Holding on to it only makes you feel guilty every time you see it. Release yourself from the guilt, and make a better choice next time.

4. "But it was free!"

Another promotional pen? Half-used hotel toiletry? Sure, thanks, you'll take it! Before you know it, all that free stuff is costing you. It takes up so much space, you need to buy organizers to hold it all. Tell yourself: Just because it's free doesn't mean it's for me. To break the habit, ask yourself, "If I had to pay cash for this, would I still bring it home?"

5. "But it's still good."

That framed art that used to hang on your wall is now hidden away in the back of the closet. Is it still good? Sure. Do you need it? Not so much. But it feels wasteful to throw it away. Tell yourself: Keeping things that are still good but no longer good for you is more wasteful than giving them to someone who could use and will appreciate them.

6. "But Grandpa would have fixed this."

The sad truth is it often costs less to buy a new one than it would to repair it. And the art of fixing things has been lost. Tell yourself: I'll research if I can fix this for a reasonable price in the next ten days; otherwise, toss it and move on.

7. "But it's too special to use."
The candy dish that might break. The china platter that needs to be handwashed. That last spritz of your favorite perfume. Tell yourself: Items are meant to be used and enjoyed. If it is too much work to maintain it, then maybe it isn't right for you anymore.

8. "But it reminds me of…"
Your home is filled with objects that have memories attached to them. The memory isn't inside the item; the item simply jogs your memory. Tell yourself: If I have to maintain all these reminders of old experiences, I won't have time for new adventures.

9. "But it was a gift."
"What if my mom finds out I gave away that sweater she gave me?" Might she be disappointed? Possibly. But I think she'd be equally, if not more, disappointed to learn you were letting it go unused, so give it to someone who can use it. Tell yourself: Your part of the gifting experience was to accept the gift in the spirit in which it was intended. Then you can let it go.

10. "But this needs to go to just the right place."
Want it to go to the perfect home or dispose of it properly? Tell yourself: If I spend all my time debating where to send it, no one gets to use it.

How to Toss Things

There are many ways to toss things. Here's how to decide which option(s) will work best for you and your stuff.

Sell in person if you:
- are willing to do the work to set up and advertise a yard sale and then spend a weekend sitting outside haggling over your stuff

- have a plan to avoid bringing unsold items back into your home

- are comfortable with people picking over your stuff and handling your belongings

- don't mind selling your stuff for low prices

Trade in if you:
- know of a local store that will accept your items

- have the ability to get your items to the store

- need something from the store where you will now have a credit

Consign if you:
- have in-season, high-end, or designer items that are new or in good condition

- can wait, usually for ninety days, to see if there is a buyer

- are willing to retrieve any unsold items or forfeit them to the shop

---

Did you know?

You can locate consignment shops by zip code at thethriftshopper.com.

Sell online if you:

- are tech-savvy enough to easily navigate online sales and auction sites, post photos, and answer e-mails

- are willing to store items until they sell

- can pack and ship items when they sell

- promise you won't read the listings to buy more things

Donate if you:

- know of a charity whose cause you support that is currently accepting the item

- don't have the time to sell your items

- failed to sell your items

- know you'd be tempted to reclaim things you are saving to sell

Give away if you:

- know someone who can use the item or its parts

- can easily get the item to the person

Put outside with a sign that says "Free to a Good Home" or join the Freecycle Network (freecycle.org) if you:

- want to get rid of items quickly

- know the items are broken but might be good for parts

- can't find a way to haul large items away from your home

Recycle if you:

- have an item you aren't using but want to avoid adding to landfills

Throw out if you:

- have items that can't be used, repaired, or recycled

Did you know?

You can purchase a Bagster at your local home improvement store, fill it with trash, then log onto thebagster.com or call a pick-up. You can also rent a dumpster from your local waste-removal company.

Where to Toss Things

Now that you've decided how you're going to get rid of your stuff, it's time to get started. Here are some resources (with good user reviews) to check out for selling, trading in, giving away, donating, or recycling almost anything. The items in the top five lists here were selected based on the questions I get asked most frequently. There are many more categories of things, of course, and this information can change, so to view an up-to-date comprehensive list, go to JamieNovak.com.

Where to Sell or Trade In Almost Anything

- Amazon.com/tradein

- LetGo.com

- OfferUp.com

- Ebay.com

Top Five Things We All Have to Sell or Trade In

1. Clothes: poshmark.com

2. Furniture: UseTrove.com

3. Watches and jewelry: Sothebys.com

4. China, crystal, flatware, and sterling silver: Replacements.com/sell-to-us (800-REPLACE)

5. Electronics (e-reader, phone, camera): gazelle.com or decluttr.com

Top Five Specialty Items to Sell or Trade In

1. Car seat: Target.com annual trade-in event

2. Wedding dress: Nearlynewlywed.com

3. Video games and consoles: Gamestop

4. Designer handbag: rebag.com

5. Musical instruments and sheet music: MusicGoRound.com

Where to Donate Almost Anything

- DonationTown.org

- GiveBackBox.com

Top Five Things We All Have to Donate

1. Books and textbooks: Betterworldbooks.com or booksforafrica.org

2. Eyeglasses: UniteforSight.org or OneSight.org

3. Stuffed animals and plush toys: stuffedanimalsforemergencies.org

4. Linens: pet shelters (used for baths and to line metal cages)

5. Keys: KeysforHope.org (sold as scrap metal to raise money for charity)

Top Five Specialty Items to Donate

1. Bicycle parts: bikesfortheworld.org or p4p.org

2. Building supplies: Habitat.org

3. Suitcases: SuitcasesForKids.org

4. Medical equipment: ProjectCURE.org

5. Old photos, letters, diaries, and other papers: Archivists.org

Where to Give Away Almost Anything

- Craigslist.org (list it as free)

- Facebook.com/marketplace (list it as free)

- Freecycle.org (nonworking items okay)

- Curbside with a sign that says "free to a good home"

Top Five Things We All Have to Give Away

1. Coupons (in date or expired less than six months ago): supportourtroops.org/troopons

2. Broken or chipped coffee mugs: artofrecycle.org or organizations that will use them in mosaics or other crafts

3. Plastic utensil packets: food bank

4. Books: BookCrossing.com (Send your book on an adventure. After registering, leave your book out, with a note, for someone to find. Once the next person logs on and updates the log about the book, you can watch it as it travels.)

5. Florist vases: Local hospitals (for patients who receive bouquets)

Top Five Specialty Items to Give Away

1. Fur or fur-trimmed items: WildBunchRehab.org (used to comfort injured wildlife)

2. Birding equipment (field guides, binoculars, hiking backpacks): American Birding Association (ABA.org)

3. Graduation caps and gowns: thrift or vintage clothing store near a college campus or local theater company

4. New and gently used bras, lingerie, and swimsuits: brarecycling.com

5. Military uniforms: SwordAndPlough.com

Where to Find Out How to Recycle Almost Anything

- Earth911.com

- TerraCycle.com

Top Five Things We All Have to Recycle

1. Unusable clothing: H&M Garment Collection Program

2. Greeting cards: stjudesranch.org/recycled-card-program (St. Jude's Ranch for Children Recycled Card Program, 100 St. Jude's Street, Boulder City, NV 89005)

3. Dried-out markers and highlighters (any brand): Crayola.com/colorcycle

4. Worn-out sneakers: Nikereuseashoe.com

5. Electronics equipment and accessories (such as televisions, stereos, printers, computers, wires, cords, and more): goodwillecycle.com

Top Five Specialty Items to Recycle

1. Torn American flags: American Legion (legion.org)

2. Wetsuits: sugamats.com

3. Used, clean mascara wands: Wands for Wildlife, P.O. Box 1211, Skyland, NC 28776

4. Crayons and crayon pieces: crazycrayons.com

5. Broken holiday light strands: local home-improvement store

Keep in Touch with Me

I hope our time together doesn't end here! We'll both continue to #KeepThisTossThat together. Join me online and share your successes so I can cheer you on one toss at a time! You can ask questions and share your current project. You can find me here:

- Online at JamieNovak.com

- The 10-Minute Podcast with Jamie Novak

- Jamie Novak YouTube Channel

- Posts on Facebook.com/JamieNovak

- Tweet @JamieNovak or Twitter.com/JamieNovak

- Insta JamieLNovak or Instagram.com/JamieLNovak

- Pins at JamieNovak or Pinterest.com/JamieNovak

- Call the 24/7 Inspiration Line 1-641-715-3900 and use code 837671

- Join the Fan Club

- Tour dates listed at JamieNovak.com